Gaywood Park Schools

1939 to 1979

Michael Walker

King's Lynn

First published in Great Britain in 2018 by
K.E.S.Publications
King Edward Vll School
Gaywood Road
King's Lynn
PE30 2QB

Typeset in Times and printed by DSD Colour Printers,
King's Lynn.

A catalogue record for this book is available from the British Library.

ISBN number: 978-0-9565697-3-8

Contents

Introduction

This book is my fifth about the history of secondary schools in King's Lynn. When I retired from the headship of King Edward Vll School I decided to mark the centenary of the opening of the present building on the Gaywood Road in 1906 by writing a history of the school. 2010 was the five hundredth anniversary of the founding of the Lynn Grammar School; hence my second book which traced the history of the school up to 1903 when its name was changed to King Edward Vll Grammar School. Having written two books on what was up to 1979 a boys' school, I decided to research the history of the West Norfolk and King's Lynn High School for Girls and the work was published in 2012. Since that school merged with Alderman Catleugh School in 1979 to form Springwood High School it seemed important to write about the Alderman Catleugh Boys' and Girls' Schools which opened in 1957.

King Edward Vll School, A Centenary Celebration, Book Guild Publishing, 2005.

Diary of a Grammar School, King's Lynn, K.E.S. Publications, 2010.

West Norfolk and King's Lynn High School for Girls, 1886-1979, K.E.S. Publications, 2012.

Alderman Catleugh Schools, 1957-1979, K.E.S. Publications, 2016.

This history of the Gaywood Park Schools from 1939 to 1979 completes the picture of secondary education in King's Lynn up to the time when the secondary schools in the town became comprehensive. As well as describing the development of the schools in terms of numbers on roll, the growth of the buildings, important events, organisation and curriculum, examination results, extra-curricular activities and the influence of the head teachers and staff, I have tried to identify students who were successful, whether it be academically, in sport or in other spheres of activity. Unfortunately it is impossible to mention every former student or teacher and inevitably many who deserve a mention will have been omitted. In some cases the Christian names of pupils may be misspelled if they have been supplied by school friends or former staff; in other cases only initials and surnames are known. For any errors and omissions I apologise.

Acknowledgements

I am grateful to the staff at King's Lynn Academy for access to the Gaywood Park documents and photographs which have been preserved at the school since 1979. My thanks go to the former students and staff who have loaned me photographs and/or have written accounts of their time at the school. Hopefully the photographs and reminiscences of former students will bring the book alive for its readers. I am also grateful to the Norfolk Record Office for access to relevant documents, specifically the governors' minutes and head teachers' reports. Thanks are also due to the *Lynn News* for permission to reproduce photographs which originally appeared in the press, to Brenda Lance and Robert Fuller for their skill in improving the quality of many of the photographs, to John and Cynthia Youngman, Dr Tom Shephard, Dr Bob Rogers, Stephen King and Tony Gayton for their support in completing the project and to my wife Elizabeth and Cynthia Youngman for proof reading the manuscript. Finally my thanks goes to Dale Thorne at DSD Colour Printers for his skill in setting the text and the photographs.

Michael Walker

January 2018

1. New Schools for King's Lynn

The Gaywood Park Schools were opened in 1939 to take all the boys and girls aged 11 to 14 in King's Lynn, other than those who were at King Edward VII Grammar School, the West Norfolk and King's Lynn High School for Girls and the Lynn Covent. There had been a number of elementary schools with senior departments, namely St James's Boys', St James's Girls', All Saints' Boys', All Saints' Girls', St Margaret's Boys', St Nicholas's Boys, St Michael's, and Gaywood Mixed. Under the scheme of re-organisation St Nicholas's Boys and St James's Infant schools were to be closed and St Michael's was to become an infant school. St James's Girls' School was to have a mixed infant department.

On Tuesday 10 October 1939 the *Lynn News* carried an article headed:
Schools to be Proud of – Gaywood Park Buildings set a New Standard.

'If peace had been preserved the *Lynn News* would this week have been reporting the full-dress opening ceremony in connection with the Gaywood Park Schools. There would have been pictures of Sir Will Spens* accepting the key from the architect (Mr Norman Wheatley), and of a representative gathering on the platform, with headlines quoting striking phrases from some of the speakers and full reports of speeches in praise of this splendidly-planned, excellently-equipped range of school buildings….But peace had not been preserved' and 'the schools had opened quietly a month ago when all of us had other things to think about.'

Instead the article gives an account of a visit to the schools on a normal working day which it described as a red-letter day in the history of the schools' canteen. It said that for a month it had

A civic visit in October 1939

* Sir Will Spens was Master of Corpus Christi College in Cambridge and lead author of the Spens Report which had recommended the tri-partite split of secondary education into grammar, technical and modern schools.

Waitress service in the dining room

been providing an appetising and satisfying meal for a daily average of 200 girls, 175 boys and several teachers, but on the previous Thursday it had entertained as guests the Mayor and Mayoress (Mr and Mrs J Harwood Catleugh), members of the Lynn Elementary Education Committee and Mr H M Howard, the Divisional Education Officer. They had lunch and then an extended tour of the schools. The newspaper reported that at the end of the meal Mr Howard asked what the Mayor thought of the school dinner. In reply the Mayor said he had only one complaint, that 'the helpings had been larger than he was accustomed to.' This got a good laugh from everyone including Mrs Catleugh. The Mayor went on to say that the meals were admirably planned, excellently cooked and the service by the waitresses - twenty of the girls in white caps and aprons - was splendid. He congratulated the domestic science mistresses who planned the meals (Miss F Brown, Miss M S Fyfe and Miss L Barber), the cook (Mrs Thurston) and those who served the food. Each week the meals were varied and the cost was covered by the charge to the boys and girls of 3d per meal.

The article was also very complimentary about the buildings.

> 'The chief impression left after a visit to these well-planned schools is that everything has been arranged to make teaching easier and learning pleasanter. The classrooms, with their large glass windows, look out over Gaywood Park, disclosing broad stretches of newly-levelled playing fields…. From a distance these single-storey school buildings look long and low; inside the rooms are lofty and light….The corridors cope with the movements of 1100 boys and girls with ease, and with surprisingly little noise.'

The schools were designed as one-storey buildings because of the unsuitability of the subsoil to receive heavy loads and because there were no restrictions on the amount of land available. To avoid long cul-de-sac corridors it had been decided to enclose large central courtyards onto

An aerial view of the Gaywood Park Schools

which the classrooms faced. All the teaching rooms, except the art rooms (which had north-east aspects) faced south east to catch the maximum amount of sunshine. The potentially noisy rooms, that is the gymnasia and woodwork and metalwork rooms, were grouped together so as to exclude noise from other parts of the buildings. The washrooms and lavatories were planned so that they could be entered from the playground and also from inside the buildings.

The cost of the new secondary schools, excluding all the furniture and equipment, but including the approach road and playgrounds, was approximately £49500. A major incentive for the local council when it took the decision to build a new secondary school in 1935 was the availability of a 50% grant from central government for development projects. The facilities provided for the secondary-age children were certainly far superior to what had been available in the elementary schools and those still provided in the un-reorganised schools in the surrounding villages.

2. Three Headmasters at the Boys' School, 1939 to 1952

Gaywood Park Boys' School

Mr H B Longman

When the school opened on Monday 11 September 1939 the first Headmaster of the Boys' Department, as it was known at that time, was Mr H B Longman, who had trained as a teacher at Cheltenham College, 1902-04. He had previously been Head of the St. James's Boys' Senior School which closed in July 1939 and some of the teachers from that school transferred with him. At Gaywood Park Mr Longman was assisted by 16 staff and two student teachers. Only one of the teachers was a graduate. Of the others, 12 were qualified teachers and three, who taught physical training, woodwork and metalwork, had practical qualifications such as certificates of the City and Guilds of London Institute.

At the start of the first term there were 523 boys on roll and they were divided into four streamed classes in each of the three year groups. There were also two special classes taken by the Headmaster and the Deputy Head, Mr O L Davison, but no further explanation of these has

The Boys' School staff in 1939-40

been found. As the boys were able to leave school at the end of the term in which they became 14 years old the numbers dropped significantly during the year, for example at the beginning of the spring term 1940 there were 467 on roll and by the start of the summer term, 434. For the next few years the number on roll at the start of the autumn term was below 500 and in 1942 as low as 451.

As the war progressed a number of teachers were called up to serve in the armed forces. Of the original 1939 staff, the first to go, in November 1939, was Mr A C Gilbert, one of the two physical training teachers. A parting gift of a silver cigarette case was presented to him 'with all good wishes for a safe and speedy return.' He was followed by the science teacher, Mr E J Guy in the summer of 1940 and Mr D E Macey, who taught history and geography, in September 1940. In the spring term of 1941 the staffing was increased by three to twenty in all. The first women teachers, Miss F Hornigold and Mrs M H Turner took up their posts in the autumn term 1941. A further member of staff, Mr F H L Manning, was called up in June 1942.

Mr Longman kept a Log Book, as was the requirement at the time, in which he noted weekly attendance figures, staff absences, accidents to pupils and significant events or visits. Britain had declared war on Germany on 3 September and so regular entries in the Log Book refer to ARP (air-raid precaution) drills, the testing of stirrup pumps for use in case of fire, the checking of pupils' respirators and actual air-raid alerts. The latter often had an effect on attendance, for example in the week ending 7 June 1940, after air-raid warnings on two successive nights. On such occasions boys were kept at home the following mornings 'to make up for lost rest.'

Another reason given by the Headmaster for lower than normal attendance was 'very severe weather' in the winter months. In the week ending 26 January 1940, for example, attendance was as low as 64.2%. On the other hand in the summer term the usual reason for low attendance was the fact that many boys took time off school to work on the land, either 'legally or illegally' according to the Headmaster. Boys could apply for permits to take time off but not all did. In the week ending 24 July 1942 attendance dropped to 56.2%. However, an air raid on the Thursday night was a contributing factor.

Important events noted in the Log Book include the celebrations held jointly with the Girls' Department each year on or around Empire Day (24 May) in the presence of civic dignitaries. These usually involved the singing of patriotic songs around the flag pole erected in 1940. Earlier, on 26 April 1940, was the first of what was to become the annual King's Lynn Schools' Music Festival. It was held in the Corn Exchange and three choirs involving 75 boys from Gaywood Park attended the event. In future years it was normally held later in the school year, for example on 18 June in 1941 when a choir of 25 boys from the school took part. In the morning auditions were held as well as a mass rehearsal for a public concert which took place in the afternoon. From 1942 the Schools' Music Festival was held at the Gaywood Park Schools.

Few examples have been found of other cultural opportunities offered to the boys during the war period. One mention is of a concert held at the Girls' School in September 1940 attended by 'a selected party of girls and boys.' It was said to be most enjoyable and that the children appreciated the performance provided by a group of talented musicians from the Pilgrim Trust. The only other mention is in February 1944 when all the boys visited an art exhibition held locally and attended talks about the paintings.

One very significant event, which took place on 5 May 1941, was the official opening of the long-awaited footbridge over the Hunstanton railway line by the Mayor, Councillor J H Catleugh. The aim had been to build it before the schools were opened but this was not achieved and at the end of September 1939 the Report of the Elementary Education Committee to the Town Council said that the delay in its erection was causing 'great inconvenience to the scholars from the more distant parts of the town.' All the boys and girls 'were on parade' for the opening ceremony.

The school's first Sports Day was held on 23 July 1941. It took the form of inter-house athletics and cricket competitions. The four houses were named after well-known Norfolk men: Admiral Lord Nelson, Viscount Charles 'Turnip' Townshend, Captain George Vancouver and Sir Robert Walpole, generally considered to be England's first Prime Minister. On this occasion Townshend House won the Athletics Shield and Vancouver the Cricket Shield. Both trophies had been made in the school workshops. The presentations to the House Captains were made by the Mayor. A week later inter-house swimming races were held and Walpole House won the trophy. The Sports Day was again held at the end of the summer term 1942 but in 1943 it was decided not to hold the usual inter-house competitions because of the large number of boys working on the land. The same was probably the case in 1944 since there is no mention of a Sports Day in the records.

No references to inter-school sport have been found in Mr Longman's Log Book. However information from former pupils and photographs of school teams in the 1940s show that inter-school football and cricket matches did take place and teams were very successful. Some photographs of the King's Lynn Schoolboys' teams are included since they were largely made up of boys from Gaywood Park and coached by teachers from the school.

It is not clear whether swimming lessons were held in the summer terms of 1940 and 1941 as the

The official opening of the new footbridge in 1941

Mr Davison and Mr Steward with the 1941 School Cricket team

Mr Davison and Mr Clark with the 1942-43 King's Lynn Schoolboys' team.

first reference is in June 1942 when it was reported that they had started at the town baths. However this seems to have been the pattern from then on, for example in the week ending 28 May 1943 the classes were held between 11 am and 12 noon from Tuesday to Friday with Mr A G Skerritt in charge.

One interesting feature of these early years was that the school was open in the summer holidays for boys who wished to take part in organised games. In 1940, for example, four masters were on duty each week. This was also the case at the Girls' School.

Lessons in the 1940s were normally of the traditional chalk and talk variety. However as early as September 1939 a portable radio receiver was provided so that BBC Schools' Broadcasts could be used. The first set of instructional films was used in October and it was reported that 'the boys appreciated this type of lesson to the full.' The following May the first 'talkie films' were shown to 3rd year boys and girls. The films were about the techniques of swimming the crawl and backstroke. From September 1940 films were regularly shown on Monday and Tuesday afternoons.

No doubt the old phrase 'boys will be boys' was in use in the 1930s and 1940s. At school assembly they were regularly warned about various misdemeanours. As early as December 1939, following complaints, the boys were warned not to take holly from the nearby woods. In January the warning was about snowballing in public places. In July theft from allotments was obviously rife. A more serious warning was issued in February 1943 following an accident caused by a boy 'jumping lorries'. Discipline was maintained largely by the use of corporal punishment. Bob Hammond (1942-45) remembers widespread use of the cane and, in the case of the PT teacher, the plimsoll. 'You were also likely to be hit on the head by a piece of chalk if your attention wandered.' Nevertheless he says 'all the teachers were very dedicated and expected respect. In the main they got it and with very little hassle....They were happy days at the Park.' In 1998 John Bocking (1941-44) wrote a very detailed account of his time at the school, some of which is reproduced below:

'Mr Allen, who I remember most of all for his passion with Esperanto....was a kindly but strict teacher who managed to instil a fair amount of knowledge into our thick heads....Mr 'Jimmy' Beckett was a man with a very quiet disposition; he rarely got angry with anyone and I cannot ever recall him resorting to the cane....The headmaster in those far off days was Mr H B 'Truffy' Longman and his second in command [was] Mr O 'Olly' Davison. Quite a lot of the masters seemed to have nicknames, some of which were very obvious and others not so....Needless to say we were very careful to call them all 'Sir' to their faces for fear of chastisement, the cane being the main form of punishment then and one did not have to get far out of line to get a taste of it....Woodwork class was taken by the very talented 'Tusky' Turner who started many a youngster on the road to a career in carpentry, many of those starting an apprenticeship at Savages or local builders....Science class was taken by a Mr Steward....a very likeable teacher....I enjoyed his lessons and carried on some of the experiments at home thanks to a small chemistry set given to me by a relative....Gym I did not like at all....some of the tortures that we were subjected to did not seem necessary even in the 1940s....Handicraft lessons were taken by a Mr Haverson and on some occasions by a Mr Manning. They learned us bookbinding etc and also printing with presses and lino cutting; these practical instructions must have started many a boy into a satisfying career after leaving school. Mr Haverson was another kindly master [who] took quite a few lads under his wing who had learning difficulties.'

John Bocking also enjoyed his gardening lessons, the films shown on Monday afternoons, swimming in the summer months and especially his art lessons with Mr Beckett. He missed part of his last term as he got a job potato picking on a farm in North Wootton but he joined the Old Boys' Association and enjoyed playing billiards, table tennis, cards and board games with old school friends.

Another person who has written about his time at the school is Cyril Marsters in his book, *Boy on a Branch – A King's Lynn and Isle of Ely Boyhood (2005)*. He was at the school when it opened in 1939:

'Everything on that first day added to the sense of making a 'new beginning': the newness both of the school buildings and of all its equipment; the fact that I had left behind my junior status and had become a senior; the previously unknown faces of many of my new classmates. After we had begun to settle down at our new desks and the class master had introduced himself, partway through the morning we received a visit from the headmaster himself – a Mr Longman. It appeared that he was circulating round each classroom to welcome the boys and to tell us what to expect at our new school.

Mr Longman was a very smart man and looked very impressive but, even in those days, I thought that he looked rather 'old-fashioned'. He wore a black jacket, pinstriped trousers, and had a bow tie. At a guess I would say that he was well into his fifties. He came over as a very friendly man, but not the sort to be trifled with. Seating himself on the class master's table at the front of the class he proceeded to give us a talk, telling us a bit about our forthcoming lessons and of the new school's facilities. He ended, I remember, by giving us advice on how to learn effectively, stressing that this was not just a case of listening. There were more ways than one of getting things into our heads, he emphasised. We would listen, we would read, we would write and we would discuss and, in the practical lessons, we would be more active still by doing – all important ways, he said, of obtaining knowledge.

The facilities at Gaywood Park, compared with those at my previous school *[St James's Primary]* seemed out of this world. Those that I came to appreciate the most were the well-equipped woodwork and metalwork rooms. I had always liked playing with wood – now I had the chance to learn how to do it properly. We were shown how to plane a piece of wood to size, how to saw, and also whilst I was at the school I began to learn how to make the different joints. I can still 'see' the woodwork master, with saw in hand, demonstrating its correct use and explaining that it only cuts on the down-stroke; there was no need to force it into the work he said, for if it was sharp and correctly set as it should be, the saw would do most of the work.

Another novelty for me was the school canteen and, as I now had further to walk to school *[from South Lynn]* I was allowed to stay to mid-day dinner. We were issued with dinner tickets and the cost was 3 pence per day. I don't remember being given any choice of menu; if anything appeared on your plate which you didn't like you just had to put up with it – though this didn't bother me much as I was not a fussy eater. All the boys in our class who stayed to dinner, sat at the same long table as our class master, who was seated at its head. A couple of boys were delegated to collect the filled plates from the canteen counter and to place them on the top end of the table, from whence they were passed along until every boy had received his dinner, whereupon the master would give the word to commence eating.'

During the war staff and pupils at the school were encouraged to save for the war effort. In 'Warship week' (16-20 February 1942) the boys' contributions to the school bank totalled £102.17s.9d and those of staff £60.10s.6d. The boys also painted posters and produced models, one of which, showing a convoy being attacked by a submarine and then sunk by a corvette, was put on public display. In 'Salute the Soldier Week' (8-12 May 1944) the total subscribed to the school bank was £457.6s.6d., well above its target of £250.

In July 1941 the school held its first Open Evening. On the Thursday 3 July and Friday 4 July from 6.45 pm to 9.30 pm parents were able to visit the school and groups of boys provided displays of singing and dancing as well as demonstrations in arts and craft, science, woodwork, gardening and sports. On both evenings the Mayor addressed the parents in the school hall 'which was crowded.'

A measure of the success or otherwise of the school under Mr Longman is to be found in the HMI Report based on an inspection carried out in October 1943 and published in January 1944. It was not a good report and contrasted markedly with that written on the Girls' Department which was inspected in the same week. A summary of the report is set out below.

'There are 465 boys on roll. They are organised in 12 classes with 4 classes arranged according to ability in each of the three age groups. The staff consisted of a Headmaster, 9 men assistants, 5 women assistants, of whom three are married women who have been absent from teaching for some years, and 2 young teachers very recently from College and 2 supplementary teachers appointed as a war-time expedient to assist in the teaching of woodwork and gardening. The timetable is so arranged that the secular work is divided into 2 morning and afternoon periods of 65 minutes duration. Whilst there are undoubtedly activities which can be more effectively taught in long periods of 65 minutes there are others as the comments below show for which a period of 65 minutes is too long and results in much too leisurely a pace in teaching, slower work from the boys and in some cases boredom for both boys and teachers.'

'The schemes of work were not available in one volume. No attempt had apparently been made to set out the aims and purpose of the school and the part that every subject should play in attaining a well-defined goal. Every subject appears to be taught in isolation; there is little or no planned correlation between subjects. Except in History and Geography and the practical subjects of Art and Craft it was impossible to follow the sequence of lessons from one class to another. It was found in some cases that the teachers themselves were not sure of the groundwork on which their lessons were or should be based. The lack of cohesion was particularly evident in the teaching of English and Elementary Mathematics. The timetable revealed that except in one class English is taught by 2, 3 or even 4 teachers to the same class. Similar conditions obtain in Elementary Mathematics. Under such conditions and in the absence of full records of work done, unity and continuity of progress are well-nigh impossible.'

'It was surprising to find also that no form of terminal or annual examination has been held to test the progress made by the boys in any subject. The result is that there is no school standard of work; the standards are those of the individual teachers and vary accordingly. It must be stated however in fairness to the teachers that failure is not due to any lack of effort on their part. Some good teaching was observed during the inspection and the bookwork is in most cases well supervised. The staff work hard but their energies are to a large extent wasted because of the lack of unifying direction or guidance. The relations between the boys and the teachers are on the whole quite good and there is no evidence to show that the introduction of the women teachers has been other than beneficial.'

Detailed comments on the teaching of the different subjects were set out in the report with suggestions for improvements. There were some positive but many negative comments.

English: 'There is a lack of cohesion in the English work throughout the school. Each teacher is said to have his own scheme of work….It cannot be said that the system of training in English in the school is likely to turn out boys able to use their mother tongue with reasonable ease and correctness.'

Elementary Mathematics: 'Some very patient and conscientious teaching was observed in the teaching of Arithmetic. The lack of cohesion is however as noticeable as in the teaching of English. In general it may be said that the standard reached by the more able boys is fair, the written work in most classes reasonably neat and the work quite well supervised. Progress in the lower forms of each year group was difficult to assess. Poor attendance is undoubtedly a very serious handicap to successful teaching with the less able boys.'

History: 'History is in the hands of two teachers between whom there is effective consultation and cooperation….An attempt has been made to devise methods of study suitable to the upper and lower classes....It is not evident that sufficient attention has been paid to the teaching of boys how to study for themselves.'

Geography: 'The syllabus for the more able boys is in the main suitable; the scheme for the others is too ambitious and too formal....the value of both schemes would be greatly enhanced if more time were devoted to the study of King's Lynn itself.'

Handicraft: 'The teaching of woodwork and metalwork has perhaps suffered more than any other subjects from staff changes....The restrictions on the supply of timber and the indifferent quality of most of it impose obvious limitations on the type, quality and quantity of work that can be done. It is to the credit of both teachers that much useful work is, in spite of the difficulties, done.'

Science: 'The specialist teacher of Science left some 12 months ago and has not, because of the lack of a suitable applicants, been replaced. The result is that Science is not at present included in the school curriculum.'

Art: 'The work gives evidence of recognition of boys' interests, conscientious study and a desire on the part of the masters to make their teaching a stimulus to the boys....The main lack is in artistic sensibility caused by shortage of good examples of study.'

Craft: 'The work in general reaches a good standard of craftsmanship,'

PE Facilities: 'The school has a well-equipped gymnasium with changing rooms and showers and the school hall is also available. In addition there are about 6 acres of playing field and an open air swimming bath at a convenient distance from the school is used during the summer months.'

In the HMI report, which covers both the Boys' and the Girls' Departments, there is also an interesting section on the dining room and kitchen, part of which conflicts with Cyril Marster's memory of who served the meals:

'It has been the practice for the senior girls under the supervision of the Domestic Science teachers to lay the tables and serve the meals. This task they have done very well. Now that the increased numbers have made it necessary to have two sittings daily, the burden of waiting is perhaps more than the girls should be expected to bear alone. There seems no reason why the boys should not take their full share of dining room duties.'

While Mr Longman is not criticised by name it is quite evident that the main problem is seen as lack of leadership. At the end of January 1944, almost certainly as a result of this poor HMI Report, Mr Longman submitted his resignation as from 30 April. Since he qualified as a teacher in 1904 it seems likely that he was of retiring age and he was given a good send off at the end of the spring term. At a whole-school assembly, attended by various important guests, including Alderman J H Catleugh, the Chairman of the Education Committee, Mr Alan Sauvain, the Divisional Education Officer, and Miss K F Sherman, the Headmistress of the Girls' Department, he was presented with a number of gifts. Mr Longman recorded in his Log Book that the staff present was a splendid barometer, the boys' gift was a silver tea service, the Old Girls' Association and the Old Boys' Association jointly gave a silver hot-water jug and the staff of the Girls' Department sent a case of silver spoons. There were a number of 'felicitous speeches' and 'the function was splendidly arranged by Mr Davison.' Mr Longman died on 16 September 1962.

Four candidates were interviewed for the post of Headmaster in May 1944 and Mr Norman W Carter, B.Sc. (London) was appointed as from the start of the autumn term. In the interim Mr O L Davison was Acting Head during the summer term. Mr Norman Carter was 34 when he was appointed. Since 1940 he had been Headmaster of a small school in the mining area of West Hallam near Derby.

Mr N W Carter

During the period of Mr Carter's headship many of the activities and events which had already been established as regular features of the school calendar continued. Empire Day was celebrated each year in May, the King's Lynn Music Festival took place in either May or June and the School Sports Day and Open Evenings were firmly established as annual events. In the spring of 1947 the school held its first Speech Day and Prize Presentation and the guest speaker on this occasion was Mr Ronald Gould, the General Secretary Designate of the National Union of Teachers. He was to be General Secretary from 1947 to 1970 and was knighted in 1955.

The place of inter-house activities was even more prominent than in previous years. In the second week of the autumn term 1944, House Captains were appointed and House Assemblies held. House matches took place throughout the year and the range of competitions was expanded to include boxing as well as football, cricket and athletics. A shield for the best school work was also introduced. From December 1947 the final of the boxing tournament was held in the evening so that it could be attended by parents and guests. Earlier, in the summer of 1947, the School Sports Day was followed a week or so later by the King's Lynn Area Sports and the following week

Mr Davison and the 1948 Nelson House cricket team

by the County Sports in Norwich. This became the annual pattern of events, except that in June 1948, the County Sports Day was held on the playing fields at Gaywood Park School. Out of the 24 districts competing Lynn won all the senior trophies. Attendance at the Girls' Athletics Sports Day became the norm from the summer of 1945.

Mr Davison and Mr Carter with the 1946-47 King's Lynn Schoolboys' team

The 1948-49 Gaywood Park football team

No references to inter-school football have been found in the records until March 1949 when it was reported that the School Xl played a team from Holbeach. However, as in the early 1940s, photographs of school teams show that inter-school matches did take place and teams were very successful.

The Prefects with Head Boy, Ron Bucke, in July 1948

One change introduced by Mr Carter was the introduction of a prefect system. The first were appointed in September 1944. The photograph shows the prefects in July 1948 with the Head Boy, Ron Bucke, in the centre. Ron was a very keen sportsman and was captain of both the school and King's Lynn Schoolboys' teams in 1947-48.

Another major innovation came, according to Mr Carter's Log Book, in January 1949 with the inaugural meeting of the Army Cadet Force. This information is somewhat puzzling as I have in my possession a photograph which shows a very large cadet group, under Acting Captain Percy Wisker, and including members of Hackney Downs Grammar School and South Wootton units which were said to be part of the Gaywood Park Army Cadet Corps. Since boys from Hackney Downs, who were evacuated to Lynn during the War, left in 1945 the school cadet corps must have existed before 1949.

Having noted the criticism in the 1944 HMI Report there were firm attempts to improve assessment of pupil progress and the co-ordination of schemes of work and teaching methods. In May 1945 the first school examinations were held and the following month pupil reports were written and sent home together with an invitation to attend an Open Evening in July. This was attended by some 300 parents and guests. In the spring term of 1946 a special meeting of the history teachers was held to discuss schemes of work and similar meetings, often in the presence of the Headmaster, were held at intervals for other subject teachers. In February 1948 subject collaboration was extended to include staff in contributory primary schools when a meeting was held of teachers of mathematics 'to discuss methods and attain uniformity.'

After the end of the war teachers who had joined the armed forces began to return to the school. Of those on the original staff the first to be re-employed, in October 1945, after five years in the Royal Navy was Mr E J Guy who taught science. As a result of his absence the HMI Report published in January 1944 had highlighted the fact that science was not included in the school curriculum.   Mr F H L Manning and Mr D E Macey returned to work in January and February 1946 respectively and Major A C Gilbert recommenced duties in May after nearly seven years in the army. Two other teachers who had joined the school after the start of the war and been called up, Mr H C Allen and Mr M Radler, also returned to the school.

After the end of the war the number of educational visits increased. As early as June 1945, Mr Gray and Mr Haverson took a party of second year boys to Castle Acre and in September and October there were trips for third years to Bircham Aerodrome. In 1947-48 after the raising of the school-leaving age to 15 and the allocation of boys to three classes related to specific vocational pathways: 4A (agriculture); 4E (engineering); and 4T (trades), visits became an integral part of the curriculum for these fourth year boys. In January 1948, for example, 4A began a series of visits to its adopted farm and in September 1948 4E and 4T visited a model-railway exhibition in Spalding. Trips of a more general nature also took place. On Thursday 15 July 1948, for example, school visits took place to Lord's Cricket Ground, Whipsnade Zoo, Lowestoft, Cambridge, Norwich and Great Yarmouth. The boys who went to Lord's saw a Gentlemen versus Players match in which legends of the game, Len Hutton and Dennis Compton, played. A memorable occasion indeed. The photograph shows Mr Carter, Mr Beckett and the boys outside the Grace Gates. The following summer the first whole-school outing took place on 27 May 1949, departing at 7.40 am and returning at 8.44 pm. The destination however is not known.

A trip to Lords' Cricket Ground in July 1948

The cultural life of some of the boys was greatly enhanced in this period by regular attendance at concerts and recitals in the Assembly Rooms at the Town Hall, for example in September, October and November of 1946 and in February, March and April 1947 concerts were attended by some 60 boys. There were also visits to exhibitions in the town and talks by visiting speakers. In November 1946, for example, Martyn Wright from the Arts Council gave talks to three classes on modern painting.

At the end of the Christmas term each year there was some form of entertainment provided for the boys. In 1946 Mr A A Gray wrote and produced a pageant that was very well received. Half of the boys watched it on Wednesday 17 December and the other half on Friday 19 December. On the Thursday evening there was a public performance attended by parents and guests including Major J Wise, the local Member of Parliament. It is however the only reference to drama which has been found in this period.

Attendance during the post war-period was in general higher than earlier in the decade. On several occasions record attendance was reported: 93.1% in February 1945; 94.3% in September 1945; and 95.6% in September 1947. However lower than normal attendance caused by bad weather in the winter and the farm-work scheme in the summer was still a problem. And for the first time, in June 1947, the Headmaster commented on the fact that attendance was affected not only by agricultural employment but also by parents taking children on holiday. That certainly is a factor in schools today.

As mentioned above the school-leaving age was raised from 14 to 15 from 1947 and so the number on roll in the school increased significantly. It jumped from 460 in September 1946 to 558 the following September and to 629 at the beginning of the autumn term 1948. There were 16 classes in September 1947, including a first-year remedial class. As indicated above the new fourth year was organised into three vocational classes. Approximately half the time was spent on basic subjects but related to the vocational courses being followed. The classes in the first three years continued to be streamed by ability.

In June 1948 the school was subject to another full inspection by Her Majesty's Inspectors of Schools. The report was much more positive than that which followed the inspection in 1943 and a summary is set out below.

'This school of 558 boys accommodates all Modern School boys resident in King's Lynn, save a few who elect to remain at one Voluntary all-age school. Additional places, totalling about one fifth of the annual four-form entry are filled at parents' request by boys from un-reorganised rural areas.'

'The aims formulated by the Head Master, and interpreted by the staff....comprise formulation of character, social training, and the full exercise of their pupils' mental powers, in addition to imparting knowledge and training in practical skills. Achievement of such aims is dependent upon the goodwill and effort of the staff. The School is fortunate in its Head Master, a man gifted with clear vision, understanding and power of leadership, under whose guidance in the last four years the School has advanced steadily towards its chosen objectives. His twenty-two qualified assistants, who co-operate loyally, compose a staff of average teaching ability and include a few accomplished teachers. The untiring support that they give as a team to the Head Master ensures results which are satisfactory in most fields and creditable in some....As the opportunity offers, the teaching power of the staff will no doubt be strengthened. Future appointments should take account of the lack of teachers with a specialist qualification in Religious Instruction, Biology and Art.'

'For the first three years....the four streams are graded by ability....Schemes of work rightly advocate variation in content and methods between the different streams....Basic subjects were taught by Form

Masters except in the 'A' stream where most teaching is specialised. Practical subjects.... are in specialist hands throughout. The slower steams devote more time to practical work than the quicker, which include in their course a language – French in the 'A' and Esperanto in the 'B' stream, the former taught by a qualified graduate. Their introduction is too recent to assess their value. An artificial language, however...cannot be deemed a suitable classroom subject for pupils of this age. Music is being developed as an integral part of the life of the school. This organisation holds a proper balance both between academic and practical subjects and between general and specialist teaching.... A Retarded class is admirable in purpose but to justify itself fully its work must become more truly remedial.'

'Progress since the issue of the last Inspection Report has been considerable. Many of the staff demand, and by constant effort secure, high standards. Much good work is now found in all subjects.... In general the boys work with interest and application, and the ready response and habit of effort now prevalent in the 'A' stream is especially gratifying.'

Comments on individual subjects are in general positive and the high standards of workmanships in the practical subjects are singled out for praise. The fact that music was being developed as an integral part of the life of the school was another strength: 'The cultural life of the school is profiting by the ably directed and widely-drawn music scheme.' The report stated that even more co-ordination of teaching both within subjects and between specialist and general subject teachers would be beneficial.

The HMI considered the fourth year separately since an experimental approach had been adopted. Grouping by ability had been abandoned and there were three classes following courses in Engineering (4E), Trades (4T) and Agriculture (4A). Approximately half the time was spent on basic subjects but related to the vocational courses being followed. Good use was made of local resources for visits and case studies. The comments in the report were positive but it was suggested that some of the brighter boys suffered from the lack of grouping by ability and that a way should be found to introduce this for the teaching of the basic subjects.

The report commented positively on the corporate life of the school as promoted by the daily assembly, the house and prefect systems, the programme of visits and wide range of hobbies pursued. It also said that Open Days and other contacts were establishing good relations with parents and former pupils.

One major criticism was the lack of an adequate library, although excellent work was being done by staff in training boys in the use and enjoyment of books. Similarly the state of textbooks called for urgent attention. 'Throughout the school they are out-of-date, of mediocre quality, insufficient, and frequently in tattered condition....generous restocking is urgently required.'

The report concluded that,

'The school is a vigorous, happy and responsible community in which Masters and boys work together for the common good. The bearing of the boys is polite and friendly, and there are many signs of their growing initiative and self-respect. Wise leadership and loyal effort have produced a community healthy in all essentials. On these foundations work of high quality may well arise.'

In view of the very positive assessment of his ability it was unfortunate that the Headmaster was not to remain for a longer period at the school. At the end of the summer term 1949 Mr Carter left to take up a new post in Brighton. Mr O L Davison was again to be the be Acting Head as the new Headmaster, Mr W Emrys Davies, B.A., BSc., M.Ed., did not take up his post until the second half of the autumn term.

Dr W Emrys Davies

Before coming to King's Lynn Mr Emrys Davies was head of the research and information department at the National Union of Teachers and previously had been a headteacher in Manchester for eight years. The most surprising feature of this headship is the short length of time that he stayed at the school. He took up his post at the start of the second half term in the autumn of 1949 and left at the end of the spring term 1952, less than three years in all. Perhaps he just saw the post as a stepping stone to better things. He was regularly absent for meetings in London as he was a member of both the NUT Consultative Committee and of the Council of the Bureau of Foreign Affairs. He also gained a Ph.D. in the summer of 1950 and this was officially conferred on him by the University of London in February 1951. It has been suggested that he spent a great deal of his time when he was at school writing his thesis!

At the beginning of the autumn term of 1949 there were 644 boys on the roll. As in previous years the numbers fell during the year as boys left at Christmas and Easter. By 1 April of 1950, when a half-yearly return was made to the Local Education Authority, the roll was down to 587 and for the next few years, even at the start of the autumn term, the number did not reach 600. In the photograph of the staff in the summer term of 1951 are the 26 teachers, Mr Horace Carter, a craft technician and Miss Ruth Simmons, the school secretary.

The Boys' School staff in 1951

However during his time at the school it continued to develop the range of opportunities offered to pupils. In his first week a County Music Adviser, Mr McKenna, took the first of a series of lessons with members of the newly-formed brass band playing instruments loaned to the school by the Local Education Authority. It is not clear whether or not the new Headmaster had played any role in getting this off the ground but he certainly must have had an interest in the value of music in education as groups of some 40 boys continued to attend the monthly concerts held at the Town Hall. In July 1951 the King's Lynn Grand Opera Group performed in the school hall.

There was also an increase in visits to the theatre and a school drama society came into being. In March 1950 two groups went to a performance of *Pride and Prejudice* at the Girls' School and at the end of that term the boys' drama group put on two public performances - although the title of the play is unknown - in aid of the Guildhall Restoration Fund. All the boys had the chance to watch the dress rehearsals. At the end of the summer term 1950 four classes put on one-act plays which were seen by the whole school. The following March the school dramatic society put on three one-act plays on two evenings.

Of particular note was a pageant on the St George's Guildhall, written and produced by Mr A A Gray, a former member of staff, and performed by a cast of about 60 boys and girls on two days in December 1950. In April 1951 40 boys from the school took part in a performance of *Jerusalem* as part of the Festival of Britain celebrations in the town. The rehearsal was recorded by the BBC and the arrangements for marking the Festival of Britain in King's Lynn were the subject of a radio programme broadcast on 1 May, entitled *The job in hand – our town*.

The first trip to a performance at the Theatre Royal in Norwich was in June 1950 when 183 boys saw *A Midsummer Night's Dream* performed by the Young Vic Company. As mentioned above, the school had raised money - £145 in all - towards the restoration of the St George's Guildhall and when it was officially opened by HM The Queen in July 1951, the Head Boy attended the ceremony. The day after its re-opening some 60 boys saw a performance of *She Stoops to Conquer* by the eighteenth-century playwright Oliver Goldsmith. And in the following September there were visits to the Guildhall to see *Bonaventure* by Charlotte Hastings and *Black Chiffon* by Lesley Storm. The latter was performed by the Caryl Jenner theatre group which specialised in productions for

children. Also in September some 25 boys attended a lecture at the Guildhall by naturalist Peter Scott and in November 1951 53 boys saw a production of *Twelfth Night*.

Other visits also extended the range of experiences offered to the boys. In February 1950 class 3A went to see an exhibition of paintings and sculpture from Cyrene at the King's Lynn Museum. The following month four classes had the opportunity to see an exhibition on Africa at St. Faith's Church in Gaywood. In June 120 boys attended the Royal Norfolk Agricultural Show, held that year at Anmer, and the

A trip to the Festival of Britain in 1951

following month there were two visits to the Town Hall to see the Treasures of King's Lynn, on each occasion involving some 200 boys. Talks by visiting speakers included ones on India, on Mauritius and on Borneo in February, and on Burma in March 1952.

The only information recorded by Dr Emrys Davies on major school trips relates to that which took place on 21 June 1951 to the Festival of Britain on the South Bank in London. 266 boys and 23 staff took part.

An interesting example of community involvement took place in April 1952 when the boys from the school attended a tree-planting ceremony on the Lynn Road in Gaywood. The aim was to teach them to respect trees on the housing estates, many of which has been vandalised in recent years. The idea had been suggested by Dr Emrys Davies. Norman Croxford and Kenneth Hayes were among 18 boys, one from each of the forms in the school, elected to help plant the trees, which were two-year old saplings of flowering cherries. To give the boys a sense of ownership their names were tied to the trees. Unfortunately only two of these trees have survived. They can be seen on the opposite side of the road from the Jet Garage and one of them, photographed in the spring of 2017, is shown on the back cover of this book.

The 1949-50 Gresham House football team

Inter-house competitions continued to flourish and in March 1952 there is the first mention of a cross-country competition in which some 400 boys took part. Sometime during the second half of the 1940s two new houses had been created, Leicester and Gresham, named after Lord Leicester of Holkham and Sir John Gresham, the founder of Gresham's School in Holt. Gresham House won the football shield in both 1948-49 and 1949-50 and also the athletics shield at the Sports Day in

The 1950-51 School football team

May 1951. The captain of the 1949-50 football team was Albert Boughen and to his right in the picture is Nigel Brown who provided it. The staff are Mr Fitheridge on the far left and Mr Lockley on the far right. At the swimming gala held in July that year Leicester House came out on top. According to J E Smith (1947-51) house points were also awarded for classwork and on a large shield at the back of the hall a running total of points was kept. The only mention found of inter-school sport in this period comes in June 1950 when a school team won the King's Lynn Junior Football Shield at Downham Market. The teacher on the right is Mr Haverson but the name of the other is not known.

The Headmaster was clearly interested in curriculum development. In the summer term of 1951 there were a number of staff meetings devoted to the discussion of specific topics – the teaching of less-able pupils, social studies, English language and mathematics. In the autumn term there were meetings to discuss the teaching of science and the 'topic method.' His reputation was such that in July 1951 he was invited to give a lecture on a course for teachers organised by the London University Institute of Education at Southlands College.

Courses in the fourth year tended to be biased towards jobs that were available in the local area and were as practical and hands-on as possible. For example, in 1950 a tractor was built in school under the guidance of Mr Lewis Turner and Mr John Gaukroger, a project of considerable interest to boys who hoped to get jobs as mechanics in garages or to work in farming. The boys cannibalised the parts from two old Austin 7 cars to provide the engine, gear box, chassis, wheels and axle. The photograph shows the completed tractor. The project prompted 13 year old David Bretton to build his own tractor from scrap materials on his father's farm.

As in previous years careers advice on job opportunities for school leavers was provided each term. General talks by local careers officers for the boys and their parents were followed up by individual interviews. There were also visiting speakers who promoted particular careers. For example in October 1950 3rd and 4th year boys visited the Army apprentice-tradesmen's display van on the school site and later in the month there was a talk for 4th years on prospects in the Royal Air Force.

One member of staff who continued his links with the armed forces through membership of the Territorial Army was Major A C Gilbert. On several occasions he was granted leave of absence to take part in guards of honour: in June 1951 at Buckingham Palace on the occasion of a state visit by King Haakon of Norway; the following month in King's Lynn when HM The Queen officially opened the newly-restored Guildhall; and on 11 February 1952 following the death of King George V he was on duty at Wolverton Station. On that occasion some 50 boy scouts who were members of the school had leave to attend the proceedings at Sandringham and when the Royal Train took the King's body back to London the whole school assembled on the playing fields to pay its respects.

An agriculture class in the late 1940s or early 1950s

The summer of 1951 saw the retirement of the Deputy Head Mr Oliver Davison who had been at the school since it was opened and Acting Head on two occasions. Before joining Gaywood Park he had been Headmaster of the All Saints' Boys' School and had taught in King's Lynn for over 40 years. A special presentation was made to him at the Speech Day in July when the guest of honour was Sir Fred Clarke, the Director of the Institute of Education in London from 1936 to 1945. Mr Davison's replacement as Deputy Head was Mr Ronald J Auchterlonie.

Less than a year later Dr Emrys Davies left the school for a new post as Education Officer to the Central Council for Health Education. At the final assembly of the spring term 1952 he was presented with a silver-plated tankard, made in the school workshops, by Kenneth Symond on behalf of the 4th year boys, with a work table, made by Mr Carter, the workshop technician, and with a pipe from the staff and the rest of the school. He was succeeded by Mr F L Kerrison Jones M.A. who was to be the Headmaster for the next eleven years.

David Bretton and a tractor built in school in 1950

3. Miss K F Sherman – a complete Headmistress, 1939 to 1951

Miss K F Sherman

Unlike the boys, the girls were to have only one Headmistress in the period up to the end of 1951. Miss Kate Sherman, who had previously been Head of the St. James's Girls' Senior School, became Headmistress of the Girls' Department of the new Gaywood Park School when it opened in September 1939. She was to be in charge for the next twelve years. There were 503 girls on roll in that first term together with sixteen members of staff and one student teacher. The numbers fell at both Christmas and Easter each year since girls left at the end of the term in which they became 14 years old. They also fluctuated from year to year. The lowest numbers were in 1945-46 when there were only 403 girls at the start of the year and this fell to 308 in the summer term, the lowest number on record. When the school-leaving age was raised to 15 in 1947 the roll went up significantly. It jumped from 408 in September 1946 to 494 the following year and to 663 in September 1949.

The teaching staff 1939-40

It was tragic that the opening of the new school coincided with the start of the Second World War. Almost the first entry in Miss Sherman's Log Book is the following poignant comment:

> 'It is unfortunate that this magnificent building has opened when the war between Germany and the Allies (Gt. Britain, France and Poland), so long avoided, has become a reality.'

Not only would the school have to deal with all the usual issues but it would also have to cope with shortages of all kinds, air raid warnings and actual raids, as well as the fact that fathers of some of the girls and husbands of staff were in the armed forces, with all the worries that entailed. However the Headmistress seemed to manage everything with a positive attitude and unfailing cheerfulness.

Miss Sherman was always keen to welcome visitors to the school. As mentioned in the introductory chapter, as early as Thursday 5 October 1939 the Mayor and Mayoress, the Divisional Education Officer and some twelve members of the Education Committee had lunch in the school canteen, with the 200 or so girls who normally stayed, and later had a tour of the school. In the week of 11-15 December over 1000 parents and other visitors took the opportunity to see the school at work. These open days were held instead of an official opening 'which the war had made impossible.' At the end of term Christmas parties for the girls were held on three afternoons and again civic visitors were invited. This was very much the custom in future years.

A Christmas party in 1949

As early as that first term in 1939 the girls were involved in supporting the war effort. In November a set of woollen articles for Lynn servicemen had been knitted and was sent to the local Comforts' collection depot. In January 1940 girls working with Miss F Brown and Miss L Barber were making warm garments for evacuees and other poor children, using material provided by Councillor Catleugh. The following month a tuck shop was opened, the profits from which would be used to buy wool for the knitting groups or for school funds. One further example of support for the war effort was specifically at the Mayor's request; in April 1940 a group of girls under Miss E G Cremer were involved in making over 130 holdalls for Air Raid Protection workers. And in May the *Youth*

Group of Service had its first meeting at which various sections were set up: Red Cross; current events; French; and knitting. Many of the staff volunteered to help and 174 girls joined the different groups. The Red Cross detachment would be very active over a number of years under the leadership of Miss Cremer.

A Red Cross contigent in 1941

The school hall became a regular venue for fund-raising events. For example In February 1940 Lady Fermoy and Prince Chavchavadze gave a piano recital in aid of the Norfolk Red Cross and the Old Girls' Association (OGA), which was already in existence, organised a whist drive and dance to raise money for wool to be used by the knitting circles. In March a radio was sent to the 7th Norfolk Regiment by the OGA. The following month the domestic science staff put on four well-attended demonstration classes on war-time cookery.

In the summer term of 1940 several events took place which were to become regular fixtures in the school calendar, as was also the case with the Boys' School. Some 75 girls, organised as three choirs, took part in the first King's Lynn Schools' Music Festival in April. In future years it would be more commonly held in May and from 1941 would be held at the Gaywood Park Schools. The normal pattern was for auditions to be held in the Boys' School in the morning and a concert, open to the public, was held in the afternoon at the Girls' School. At the Empire Day celebrations on 24 May 1940 members of both schools, in the presence of the Mayor and other civic dignitaries, assembled around the newly-erected flag pole and sang patriotic songs. Miss Sherman proudly wrote in her log that 'every girl wore uniform on this day.'

Also in May 1940 the first inter-house netball matches took place. Near to the beginning of the autumn term the girls had been divided into six houses: Balmoral; Buckingham; Glamis; Marlborough; Sandringham; and Windsor. The names of all the houses have clear links to royal residences. On this first occasion the competition was won by Glamis and all the girls were allowed to watch the first and the final matches. The first inter-school match took place in June. It was

Empire Day celebrations

against a team from Mansford Street Girls' School in London who had been evacuated to the area. They beat the Gaywood Park team by 12 to 2. Miss Sherman acknowledged that they were 'superior in passing' but she also made the telling comment that 'they interpreted the rules differently from us.' In the return match the Gaywood Park loss was even heavier - by 16 goals to 2.

Another wartime necessity was to provide home-grown produce and so a kitchen garden was developed at the school. The photograph shows girls at work. In June 1940 Miss Sherman recorded that 'garden peas from the school garden were enjoyed at dinner today' and that 'radishes and onions are being used for salad in the canteen.' A week later there is a similar entry in her log: 'Broad beans from the garden were enjoyed at dinner today.'

Unlike the log written by Mr Longman of the Boys' School, Miss Sherman makes relatively few references to air-raid practices. However on 10 July 1940 she mentions the first of a series of lectures on 'What to do in an air raid' being given in the school hall to about 100 local residents. This was followed by some remarks by the Mayor and an ARP practice by the school. Three teams of girls demonstrated the use of stirrup pumps.

At the end of that first year the school closed on 26 July. A quarter of the staff were on duty each week for a special course of games and recreational activities, but it in the event only a small percentage of the girls availed themselves of the opportunities. Also during the holidays great quantities of plums were made into jam or bottled fruit by the domestic science teachers. By 29 August the canteen had received 325 Kilner jars of bottled plums and 485 lbs of plum jam. There was a similar arrangement in the summer holidays in 1941 and Miss F Brown with the help of the mistresses on duty preserved a quarter of a ton of plums and 110 lbs of runner beans for use in the canteen.

Digging for Victory

An air raid practice in July 1940

At the beginning of the autumn term in 1941, 1942 and 1943 the big push was on the collection of blackberries. On 15 September 1941, for example, 30 girls with Miss F Brown and Miss L Bunkle went on an excursion by bicycle to gather blackberries. They returned with 74 lbs of fruit which together with apples, which were donated, was made into 91 lbs of blackberry and apple jam and 26 lbs of bottled blackberries. Other expeditions took place that month and in all some 2 cwt of fruit was collected for use in the canteen over the winter. The following September the domestic science teachers made 597 lbs of blackberry and apple jam, 150 lbs of jelly, 42 lbs of plum jam and 220 bottles of plums in 3 and 4 lb jars. These are quite staggering amounts. The work rate must have been phenomenal.

The school operated as normally as was possible during the war. Lessons at that time were largely chalk and talk but the showing of educational films became a regular feature of school life. At the beginning of September 1940 a programme of what were called 'talkie cinema' films began and continued throughout the year. These were shown in the Boys' School hall. In future years films were shown once or twice per month and Miss Sherman regularly recorded the fact that the whole school had been 'to the cinema at the Boys' School.' For example, on 28 October 1941 there were four films: on the cultivation of tea; on cane sugar production; on raw materials; and on the involvement of Indian troops in the war. Sometimes the films were rather more entertaining, for example in December 1942, as a Christmas treat, the girls watched *Mickey Mouse, Popeye* and *The Ghost goes West*. Adventure stories such as *King Solomon's Mines* and *The Scarlet Pimpernel* were occasionally shown. Sometimes groups of girls were taken to the Majestic Cinema to see classic films such as *Great Expectations* in March 1947 or *Hamlet* in December 1949.

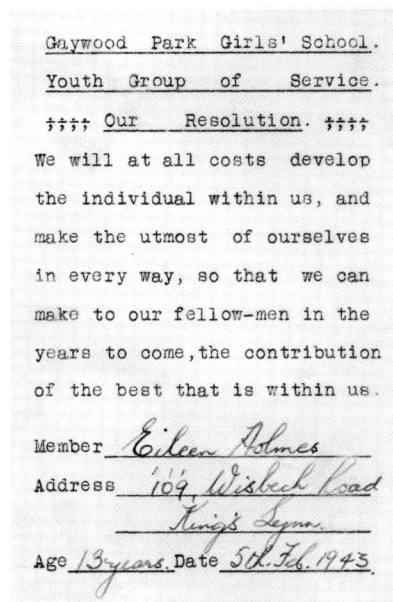

Gaywood Park Girls' School.

Youth Group of Service.

✝✝✝ Our Resolution. ✝✝✝

We will at all costs develop the individual within us, and make the utmost of ourselves in every way, so that we can make to our fellow-men in the years to come, the contribution of the best that is within us.

Member *Eileen Holmes*

Address *109, Wisbech Road*

King's Lynn.

Age *13 years.* Date *5th Feb. 1943*

A Youth Group of Service card

There were continuing examples of charity fund-raising and ways of supporting the war effort. The Youth Group of Service mentioned above organised a salvage campaign and sent the results to various depots. In November 1940 they held a Bring and Buy bazaar which raised £3.6s. 6d, most of which was sent to the BBC in response to Uncle Mac's appeal on the radio for funds to purchase a mobile x-ray unit. In future years the sums raised for charity were rather larger, for example in November 1941 a Bring and Buy bazaar raised £20.18s. which was sent to the Help to Russia Fund and the local Comforts' Fund. Miss Sherman called this 'an amazing result.' As in the Boys' School, national savings was heavily promoted and there was an annual savings week. By February 1941 there were 441 members of the school's saving groups and over £200 had been deposited; in April 1943 the total had reached £1050.5s.

Cultural opportunities were limited but on 24 September 1940 a group of girls and boys listened to a 'beautiful' programme of music provided by Miss Anne Wood, who had organised the first King's Lynn Music Festival the previous April. On 6 November some girls gave a performance of dance and song in the Town Hall in aid of the Mayoress's Comforts' Fund. In school, music and drama productions in the early years usually took place at the end of the autumn or spring term. In December 1941, for example, Miss Bunkle's form put on a Nativity play while another first-year form, prepared by Miss K Spinks, performed scenes from *A Christmas Carol*. There was a special evening performance for parents. The following April two school plays were performed: *The Story of Persephone*, produced by Miss G M Williams with music by Miss D Freeman; and the school-room scene from *Quality Street*, produced by Miss L Bunkle. As well as performances for the Girls' and Boys' Schools there were two evening performances when, according to the Headmistress, the audiences were 'large and appreciative.' These plays were put on in aid of war charities. £35 was sent to the Comforts' Fund for POWs and £12 to the local Red Cross.

A production of Quality Street in 1942

As the dangers of fire bombs increased in February 1941 a rota of staff was organised to sleep on the premises as fire watchers. There were 16 volunteers so with two on each night, including Saturday and Sunday, the duty came round every eight days. The very real danger from incendiary bombs was demonstrated on the night of 29-30 June 1942 when the roofs of the north and south blocks and of the main hall of King Edward VII Grammar School on the Gaywood Road were hit. The following morning the Gaywood Schools' canteen provided breakfast for the 27 boarders and four boarding-house staff from K.E.S.

Although none of the teachers at the Girls' School went to war some of their husbands were in the armed forces. Miss Queenie Hall who was on the staff from September 1939 had special leave of absence to get married at the end of September 1941. On her return she was presented with a silver-plated tea pot, cream jug and sugar bowl by the staff. Her husband, Mr Geoff Williams, was later to be taken prisoner by the Japanese. This was a very worrying time for Mrs Williams and she was greatly relieved when news came on 11 September 1945 that he was safe and would soon be returning home. The message came through to Miss Sherman who went straight into Mrs William's class with the good news. When her husband got home in October Mrs Williams was granted six week's leave of absence on compassionate grounds. She left the school on 30 September 1946 but for several years was a regular supply teacher and she was re-appointed to the staff as from November 1950. Mrs Williams worked at the school until she retired in July 1976.

Throughout Miss Sherman's time at the school there were often staff shortages and periodically the normal timetable had to be modified or even abandoned, as was the case for two weeks in November 1941. On a more positive note, Miss Sherman wrote in her log on 14 December 1942, 'We are fully staffed for the first time since September 14th.' One can almost hear the sigh of relief. One good piece of news on the staffing front was that the Education Committee agreed to appoint Miss L Bunkle (later Mrs Gee) as Second Mistress as from 1 November 1941, with a special responsibility allowance of £20 per year. She left at the end of the Christmas term 1943 and was succeeded as Second Mistress by Miss G M Williams, albeit not until September 1944. For four weeks at the beginning of the autumn term 1947 Miss Sherman was in the United States to attend a conference and to visit some relatives. During that time Miss Williams was Acting Head. Earlier in 1947 the staffing position was again bad. In a letter to Mrs Queenie Williams (dated 30.1.47) she says that 'staffing is a gruesome business and is worsening daily. If only we could make replacements I wouldn't mind, because the circumstances are inevitable, but when no response comes after months of adverts then indeed the hope deferred makes the heart sick.'

22 September 1941 saw the first of what was to be an annual Harvest Festival Service. Produce from the school garden and bread baked in the domestic science rooms were on display. In future years the produce was usually brought in from home by the girls. Miss Sherman describes a magnificent display of fruit, vegetables and flowers and 'anything from a pumpkin to an egg,' in October 1942. For several years the produce was taken after the service to the hospitals but by 1949 the main beneficiaries were the Gaywood Old Folks' Club and various almshouses. That year the Headmistress said that 'in spite of the drought and the extraordinary summer the quality and quantity of the gifts exceeded those of all previous occasions.' From 1947 an annual Easter Service would also be held and the donations taken to the needy. In March 1949, for example, over 600 eggs and quantities of spring flowers, grapes and other fruits and produce were later taken to the Gaywood Almshouse and to the 40 members of the Gaywood Old Folks' Club.

On 15 July 1942 the school held its first Sports Day. Marlborough House won the Athletics Shield and the Victrix Ludorum Cup, donated by Councillor Catleugh, was won by Sadie Howatt. The following year school attendance in June and July was so badly affected by the number of girls working on the land that the Sports Day planned for 14 July was cancelled. The next mention of a Sports Day is in 1945 and from then on it became an annual event. In 1946 girls from the school competed in the King's Lynn Sports and in the County Sports. At the latter in Norwich 13 girls represented King's Lynn and some 40 girls and four staff went to watch. The school was closed for the day. The town gave a good account of itself and won two shields – the Fermoy Shield for the 14-16 age group and the Colman Shield for the 12-14 age group. Monica McCowen set a new record in the long jump with 14' 9". Monica and Rosemary Burrows, who had won the 150 yards race, were selected to represent the County at the All-England Athletics Championships at Eton near Windsor on 20 July. Miss Sherman said that they 'did not do anything spectacular' but 'it was a great experience for the children and well worthwhile.' In fact getting to the national finals was a major achievement.

There was more success in athletics in the coming years. In 1947 five girls were chosen to represent King's Lynn at the County Sports: Brenda Knight in the U12s; and Kathleen Featherby, Joan Flatman, Joan Gratwick and Dorothy Rains in the 12-14 age group. Joan Gratwick came 3rd in the long jump and the 12-14s relay team, which included two of the Gaywood Park girls, easily won. The following year the County Sports were held on the Gaywood Park playing fields and

King's Lynn retained the three team shields it had won in 1947, the Fermoy Shield, the Coleman Shield and the Moore Shield (for the 10-12 year olds.) Six Gaywood Park girls represented King's Lynn. Kathleen Featherby came 2nd in the 100 yards and also 2nd as part of the 13-15s relay team with Joan Flatman, Joan Gratwick and a girl from the WN & KL High School. Edna Case broke the 11-13 age group long jump record with a jump of 14' 5" and Daphne Cross won the 13-15s high jump competition and was selected to take part in the National Championships in Bath. The following year Daphne Cross was Victrix Ludorum in the School Sports and 'was crowned with a laurel wreath in classic style.' She just missed out on qualification for the National Sports at Carshalton, her jump of 14' 7" having been beaten by a girl who jumped 14' 8" in the Quadrangular Sports in Norwich.

The next very successful year in athletics was in 1951 when, according to Miss Sherman, 'Gaywood Park girls had quite outstanding success [in the King's Lynn Sports] and Eryl Dye was the first girl to receive the Allen Challenge Cup for the best performance of the afternoon.' She reduced the record time for the 15-17s 150 yards by over 2 seconds. Ann Featherby was 1st in all her events and all the relay teams won. 11 girls were selected to represent the town in the County Sports. Eryl and Ann were again placed 1st in their respective 150 yards races. Ann Featherby was an all-round sportswoman and in October of 1951 she was selected to play attacking centre in the County Netball Team.

Eileen Mott, Junior Swimming Champion in 1946 and 1947

Inter-house matches in netball were held each year at the end of the spring term or early in the summer term. The Woodwark Cup (named after the late Colonel G G Woodwark who had been Chairman of the Education Committee from 1921-38) was awarded to the winning house which later played but usually lost to a staff team. At the end of the summer term 1941 an inter-house swimming gala was held for the first time. The championship cup for the best swimmer was awarded to two girls, Betty Capps and Pamela Henry who tied for the honour. The overall winner was Marlborough House. In future years Gaywood Park girls did well in the annual King's Lynn Ladies' Swimming Club gala. In both 1946 and 1947, for example, Eileen Mott was the Junior Champion and in 1950 Julie Brown was Junior Champion and Greta Harper won the Junior Diving Trophy. The following year Margaret Simpson took both titles.

A rounders competition was also introduced in July 1941. Glamis won on this first occasion and 'great excitement prevailed when the mistresses played and easily beat the winning house team.' It was not until 1948-49 that an inter-house hockey tournament was introduced. The first inter-school match against a team of evacuees was mentioned above. It was not until after the end of the war that matches were regularly organised against other schools. At a netball tournament in May 1946 Gaywood Park girls 'easily beat' teams from Downham Market, Upwell and Terrington but in a rounders match against the Girls' High School in July honours were even; the U15 team lost but the U14 team won. In 1946-47 there were netball matches against Fakenham and Downham Market and on each occasion the two Gaywood Park teams won. There was similar success in a rounders tournament in June when the school won all their matches against six other teams. The following year the school was less successful, the 1st team losing to the Lynn Convent at rounders in the autumn term and both teams losing at netball in the spring. However within a few days of those defeats, at the beginning of March, both teams gained 1st place in a netball tournament involving five other schools. It was also in March 1948 that the school's 1st XI hockey team played it first competitive match. Unfortunately it was beaten 13-0 by Downham Market Grammar School. The school did however get its own back by beating them at netball 17-6. Over the next few years in matches against Downham the pattern was similar with the school often winning at netball and rounders but not at hockey. The hockey team's first win was against the Lynn Special Grammar School in December 1949 and the following year it gained joint 1st place in a tournament for Norfolk secondary modern schools, tying with Diss in the final.

The school's first Open Days in lieu of an official opening are mentioned above. In December 1940 the school was again open to parents on two afternoons and these attracted some 800 visitors. From 2.15 to 3.15 pm there were conducted tours to see the girls in normal lessons and exhibitions of work. Then from 3.30 to 4.30 pm a programme of song and dance was put on for the visitors in the school hall. It is not clear whether similar opportunities for parents were offered every year but there were certainly Open Days in July 1942 and in December 1945 and 1946. At the latter, as well as the normal programme of entertainment, prizes, certificates and sporting trophies were presented. In July 1948 this was taken a little further and the first Speech Day was held. In the afternoon parents were able to consult staff about their daughters' progress, there was a gymnastics display, a performance of the trial scene from Shaw's *St Joan* and some singing. In the evening there were performances from the violin class, the school choir, and groups demonstrating modern dance, folk dancing and choral speaking. The Headmistress gave a report and Lady Fermoy presented prizes and certificates. In 1949, 1950 and 1951 the Speech Day followed a similar pattern. The guest speakers in these years were respectively Mr Emrys Davies, the Headmaster designate of the Boys' School, Lady Somerleyton, and Dr Lincoln Ralphs, the Chief Education Officer for Norfolk. Of the latter occasion Miss Sherman said in her log, 'This, my last Speech Day, was a happy success and one that leaves me with the happiest of memories.' In his address Dr Ralphs had described her as 'a distinguished and brilliant headmistress.'

Music and drama continued to develop during and after the war. In November 1943 a violin class under Mr S Phillips of Clenchwarton was started. In the same month J M Barrie's *Peter Pan* was put on and the public performances on two evenings were well attended. There were also performances for local junior schools. Amy Wells, now Mrs Williamson, who was one of the lost boys still remembers her only line – 'Oh mournful day!' At the King's Lynn Music Festival the following June the school's contribution was minimal as Miss Freeman, the music mistress, had been very ill. However the violin group 'gave a good account of themselves.' At the end of the summer term 1944 Mr and Mrs Phillips entertained the school to an hour of music which included individual and group performances. As well as the violin group, a lunchtime percussion group also played. Later that year in December 1944 a Christmas Concert was put on which included performances from the choir, the percussion and violin groups, as well as a display of dance and a nativity play. There were two evening performances for parents and civic dignitaries as well as an afternoon show for the girls.

The school was fortunate to be able to attend some recitals given by celebrated musicians. In December 1944 violinist Sybil Caton was brought to the school by Lady Fermoy and in October 1945 some 300 boys and girls from various schools enjoyed a performance by pianist, Kathleen Long in the school hall. There was a public performance in the evening. At the end of March 1946

70 girls went to a piano recital organised by the Arts Council at the Town Hall. There was another such concert in May and then from September 1946 a season of monthly concerts was held each year from 3.30 to 4.30 pm on a Friday afternoon and girls from Gaywood Park attended these performances as did many pupils from the other secondary schools in the town. They were generally known as 'lunchtime concerts' not because they were held at lunchtime but because they were organised by the King's Lynn Lunchtime Concert Society. One of the most famous performers was the contralto Kathleen Ferrier who 'delighted the audience' at the Town Hall on 8 May 1948 and again in April 1950.

It was some time after the production of *Peter Pan* in 1943 that a major production was staged at the school. There were short plays put on before Christmas or on Speech Day but in December 1949 the Drama and Music Clubs entertained the school and parents with a double bill: *He That Should Come*, a nativity play by Dorothy L Sayers, produced by Miss Williams; and three excerpts from Handel's *Messiah* by the school choir, led by Mrs Richardson. The following March the Drama Club gave a matinee and two evening performances of Jane Austin's *Pride and Prejudice* to 'full and appreciative audiences.' According to the Headmistress, 'the production reached a very high standard in every way.' Alderman J H Catleugh on the first evening and Lord Fermoy on the second 'publicly complimented the performers and all concerned with the fine production.' As a result the school was able to send a cheque for £75 as a first instalment to purchase a seat in the newly-restored Guildhall. Over £100 was sent in July 1950, the proceeds of a Bring and Buy sale and entertainment provided by the Vaulting Club, the Music Club and the Puppetry Group. Finally £22 was sent in December 1950 to complete the purchase of a second seat following the performances on two days of a pageant, *The Guild of St George*, written by Mr A A Gray, a former member of staff at the Boys' School, and including a cast of some 60 boys and girls. It was produced by Miss G M Williams and Mr R J Stevenson. The Official Opening of the restored Guildhall by Her Majesty the Queen on 24 July 1951 was described by Miss Sherman as a 'Red Letter Day'. June Denny, the Head Girl, and Miss Williams, the Deputy Head, occupied the two seats purchased by the school. The Headmistress attended in her capacity as a member of the Appeals' Committee.

During the war trips from school were rare. The blackberry-collecting expeditions have already been mentioned. There were also short trips into town, for example to see the *Wings for Victory* exhibition in April 1943 at the Corn Hall or to see an exhibition of Scottish paintings at the Museum in February 1944. However after the war the number and range of trips increased significantly. The first school outing took place in July 1946 when 140 girls and 15 staff went to Castle Acre, Walsingham and Cromer, returning to King's Lynn by the coast road. There was a similar trip in June the following year. In addition, in July 1947, 86 girls went on a trip to Stratford-upon-Avon and Kenilworth Castle. They saw a performance of *Twelfth Night* and visited many of the sights of Stratford. In the summer term of 1948 there were outings to London for 4th years, to Cambridge for 3rd years, to Norwich for 2nd years, to Hunstanton for the Remove Form and one hundred 1st year girls were taken on a trip to Walsingham, Holkham Hall, Wells-on-Sea and Burnham Thorpe.

The first main residential trip was to the Lake District during the Easter holidays in 1949. Miss Sherman, Miss Williams, Miss Brown and Mrs Baker took 19 girls to Buttermere for a week. It was described as 'an unqualified success….They all looked very well in health.' In December 1949 the Headmistress proposed a trip to Paris to take place at Easter 1950 at a cost of £25. The parents of some ten girls expressed an interest in it going ahead but the staff did 'not feel equal to committing themselves' to the cost 'which would be more in the case of adults.' As a result the idea was dropped. Another residential trip took place in April 1951 when 35 girls in the 4th year,

A trip to Stratford-upon-Avon in 1947

accompanied by Miss Sherman, Miss Dunwoody, Mrs Baker and Mrs Gwynne, stayed for two nights at the Devonshire Street Club in London. As well as having a tour of the main sights such as the Houses of Parliament, Westminster Abbey, St Paul's Cathedral and the Tower of London, they saw a ballet at Sadler's Wells and a play at the Phoenix Theatre. However the major outing that year was to the Festival of Britain Exhibition. 303 girls and 41 adults, including children from the High School and St James Girls' School, travelled by special train to London on 10 May.

May 1951 was an eventful month. On 5 May some 15 pupils from schools in Lynn were taken to London by Mrs Richardson, Mr Allen from the Boys' School and Mrs Nash from the Girls' High School. They were to take part in a National Festival of Schools' Music at the Albert Hall the following day. The Royal Philharmonic Orchestra conducted by Sir Adrian Boult, the National Youth Orchestra and a massed choir of 1150 voices gave memorable performances. Similar festivals took place in future years and Gaywood Park pupils were often involved.

Trips to the theatre became a regular event. In September 1949 a small group of ten girls and three staff saw *Romeo and Juliet* at the Maddermarket Theatre in Norwich and in October some 40 girls saw *Macbeth* at the Embassy Theatre in Peterborough. In January 1950 the Young Vic Players gave two performances of *Harry of England* (excerpts from *Henry IV* and *Henry V*) and *The Anniversary* by Chekov. Over 300 children from local schools attended on each occasion. In June later that year a party of 400 girls and staff attended a matinee performance of *A Midsummer Night's Dream* by the Young Vic Players. The venue for these performances is unknown. In September 1950 members of the Drama Club saw *The Merchant of Venice* in Peterborough. After the opening of the restored Guildhall there would be many more opportunities to see plays and attend concerts in King's Lynn, for example on 25 July 1951 some 60 girls saw *She Stoops to Conquer* by Oliver Goldsmith. Theatre trips would not however be restricted to King's Lynn as mentioned above. In January 1951 a group of girls was taken to Norwich. In the morning they went to see an exhibition of children's art at the Castle Museum and in the afternoon they saw a production of *A Midsummer Night's Dream*.

THE PARKSONIAN

Gaywood Park Secondary School for Girls
KING'S LYNN.
1947.

The 1947 Parksonian

In 1947-48 the first copy of a school magazine, *The Parksonian*, was produced. It included news of the previous year's activities, articles by the girls and detailed reports on the house competitions. During Miss Sherman's last term (Autumn 1951) the fifth copy was published and she proudly announced that it was larger than usual and cost 2s. A school magazine continued to be produced for a few years under Miss Bullock but more of that in Chapter 6.

During the war apart from inter-house sport most of the extra-curricular activities were geared to some kind of service as illustrated by the Youth Group of Service and the Red Cross detachments. However in the autumn term of 1949 Miss Sherman led discussions with staff willing to help set up other after-school activities. By the end of September the following clubs were in operation: drama (including art and needlework), music, history, geography/films, science, vaulting and French.

The HMI Report of the inspection which took place in October 1943 is the only independent evaluation of progress in the Girls' School during the period of Miss Sherman's headship. It was much more positive than that produced on the Boys' School which was inspected at the same time. Perhaps that is why no inspection took place in 1948, as was the case with the Boys' School. The report which was published in January 1944 is summarised below.

'There are 460 girls on roll, organised in 13 classes. Four classes are arranged according to ability in each of the three age groups, and a special class for girls who, for various reasons, are retarded and/or backward. The object of the special or remedial class is to give the girls tuition in the basic subjects so that they can as soon as possible take their place in the class appropriate to their age. As the class was formed in September of this year the schemes of work are still in the experimental stage, and it is thus too early to assess the progress made. Some suggestions whereby the work might be made more vital and more interesting for the girls were made during the inspection.'

The domestic science room

'The staff consists of a Headmistress and 17 assistants, three of whom are fully qualified Domestic Subjects teachers.'

'The department gives an immediate good impression which is further strengthened by more detailed inspection. An atmosphere of happy co-ordinated effort, of controlled freedom, pervades the school. The girls are divided into six Houses, and in addition, every form has its Captain. In this way healthy, friendly competition is fostered and opportunities are provided for service and for training in leadership. The girls have pleasant manners, and converse readily, easily and courteously with a visitor. They obviously take a pride in themselves and their school.'

'The staff, a blend of youth and experience, and composed of teachers of diverse gifts and varying abilities, form under the skilful, tactful, sympathetic and definite guidance of the Headmistress a good and workmanlike team.'

'In drawing up the schemes of work the Headmistress has wisely consulted her staff. In general, and with exceptions mentioned below in the notes on particular subjects, the syllabuses are suitable and have been devised to meet the varying needs and capacities of the girls.'

'Tests are set at the end of every term and detailed reports are sent to the parents. In addition the Head Teacher carries out a full and comprehensive examination in all subjects once a year. All the scripts are examined carefully by the Headmistress, and reports on the results of her survey are conveyed to the teachers. This annual stock-taking is very much to be commended.'

The Report includes detailed comments on the teaching of the different subjects with some suggestions for improvement. While there were criticisms, examples of which are quoted below, overall the comments were very positive.

Elementary Mathematics: 'This subject is taught effectively throughout the school.'

English: 'The general lay-out of the work and the methods of teaching in the A classes leave little to be desired. They are the work of an inspiring and well-informed teacher of English….Dramatic work with the brighter girls is very good. A recent production of *Peter Pan* was an excellent piece of co-operative work; the English teacher, the Music mistress, one of the Physical Training staff and the Needlework teachers combined together to produce an attractive performance.'

History: 'The work arising from a school project concerning the United States of America reached a high standard in preparation and research. Visits are paid from time to time to places of local interest so that the children might be aware of the rich inheritance of this ancient borough.'

Art: 'This subject is in the hands of a gifted and competent teacher.'

Needlework: 'Much of the work shows a commendable standard of neatness and special mention must be made of embroidery based on traditional designs.'

The needlework room

PE Facilities: 'Good provision is made for this subject. A fully equipped gymnasium with changing rooms and shower baths, assembly hall, hard playground and playing fields, in a delightful setting, enable a full programme of gymnastics, dancing and games to be carried out.'

The gymnasium

However the teaching of English to the less-able girls was said to lack cohesion. 'The result of this is that a wider gulf than usual separates the brighter classes from the rest.' Comments on geography, science, craft and housecraft were mixed and music was not inspected.

On 13 January 1944 the contents of the report were made know to the staff and Miss Sherman recorded in her log that 'the whole school can feel satisfied and encouraged by the remarks.'

Memories of former pupils who were at the school in the 1940s are very positive:

'All in all I really enjoyed my time at Gaywood Park'. Dorothy Goff (Walker), 1944-47;

'My time at Gaywood Park was very enjoyable and helped me throughout my life.' Margaret Bensley (Goldsmith), 1945-49;

'I have happy memories of Gaywood Park.' Marnya Kimberley (Woods), 1947-51.

Some people remember Miss Sherman as a bit of a martinet who would walk around the school likely a 'stately galleon'. It is also said that she was a bit of a snob and showed less interest in girls from poorer families who could not afford the school uniform. However she was clearly very highly regarded by many other people. Margaret Bensley (Goldsmith) said 'she was very kind' and that 'we all had great respect' for her.'

In 1951 Miss Sherman was given a large number of gifts to mark her retirement but even before that, in March 1946, she was presented with a silver salver to mark her 25 years as a Headmistress in King's Lynn. Her first leaving present was a rather unusual one. It was given to her by Dr Emrys Davies in October 1951 on behalf of the Boys' School. It was 'a beautiful lectern' which she in turn donated to the Girls' School as a symbol of 'the friendship and cooperation between the two schools.' In November Mr and Mrs Greenacre, the caretaker and school cook, gave Miss Sherman a standard lamp as a leaving present. On 10 December there was a Civic Reception held at the Town Hall to mark her retirement. It was attended by some 400 people including distinguished guests such as Lord Fermoy. Mr Alan Sauvain, the Divisional Education Officer, spoke warmly of her work and referred to her as 'a complete headmistress.' Mr J H Catleugh, Chairman of the Lynn Divisional Executive, said that her retirement marked 'the end of an epoch.' He presented her with a gift she had chosen herself, a crocodile handbag, which he said was given with 'real love and affection of all those who had subscribed.' She was also to receive a cheque for the remainder of the money and there were presentations of flowers and a hand-bound book. Miss Sherman recorded in her log: 'The occasion gave me great happiness.' A week later in assembly the Head Girl, Joan Freestone, presented,

Miss Sherman's retirement party

on behalf of the girls, a nest of tables, a set of cut-glass goblets and a large bunch of carnations. On 19 December at the end of the 4th year party Alderman Catleugh, gave her a cheque for the rest of the money collected by subscription and 'paid me a high tribute for my work in the school.' The following day there was a concert in school after which the Music Club gave her with a bunch of red roses and at a staff party that evening the Deputy Head, Miss Williams, presented her with an illuminated scroll listing all the names of the staff and a silver and enamelled dressing-table set.

At the end of term assembly on 21 December Miss Sherman wished her successor, Miss Bullock, 'as great a happiness as it has been my privilege to derive from working at this beautiful and interesting school.'

Katherine Florence Sherman died on 14 June 1979, aged 91 years.

4. Commendable progress at the Boys' School, 1952 to 1963

Mr F L Kerrison Jones

Following the resignation of Dr Emrys Davies an appointing committee was set up to choose his successor. There were 99 applications for the post. Some 13 men were long listed for further consideration and it was decided that six would be interviewed, including the Deputy Head, Mr Auchterlonie. In the event two of the short-listed candidates withdrew and so only four were interviewed. Mr Kerrison Jones, a graduate in Mathematics who had studied at Jesus College, Oxford, was offered the post. He had begun his career at a school in York in 1924 and in the following 28 years, as well as teaching in schools, he had lectured at Wimpole Park Teacher Training College and at technical colleges on engineering and building courses. He had also spent four years in the Royal Air Force Education Service.

When Mr Kerrison Jones took up his post at the start of the summer term 1952 there were 536 boys on the roll. This rose to 570 at the start of the autumn term and there was a gradual increase to 700 in 1956. However with the opening of the Alderman Catleugh Schools in September 1957 numbers fell to 585 and this decline continued so that by 1962 the roll was down to 484. In 1952 there were 25 assistant teachers in addition to the Headmaster, all of whom were men except one, Mrs Freda Shread, who had been appointed in 1941 during the Second World War. Of the original 1939 teachers nine were still on the staff: Mr J B Beckett; Major A C Gilbert; Mr E J Guy; Mr E G Haverson; Mr D E Macey; Mr F H L Manning; Mr A G Skerritt, Mr L R Turner; and Mr P S Wisker.

The new Headmaster had an eventful first term. In July he and Miss Bullock, the Headmistress of the Girls' School, were introduced to H M the Queen Mother and Princess Margaret on the occasion of their attendance at *The Pageant of St George* performed by boys and girls from the Gaywood Park Schools on 23 July at the Guildhall as part of the second King's Lynn Festival. The producers, Miss G M Williams, Mr C C Nelson and Mr J S Waine, were also formally presented. At the end of the afternoon performance the cast and the choir lined up to form a guard of honour for the royal party. Peter Smalls played St George and Richard Mason the dragon. According to a press report, Richard was thrilled when asked by Princess Margaret to show her how the dragon's eyes lit up. He also caused much amusement when he operated the foot-long tongue which sprang from its mouth.

The term was busy with the usual range of activities such as the Empire Day celebrations, Sports Day, the King's Lynn Schools' Musical Festival, Speech Day and school outings. The trips which took place on 27 June were more varied than in the past. One group went to Whipsnade Zoo, another to Cromer and the third to London. On the London trip some boys went to Battersea Park and the rest to a cricket match at Lords to see the MCC versus Oxford University.

The Pageant of St George in 1952

In September 1952 the school held its first meeting for the parents of new pupils. This is common practice in schools today but was quite an innovation at the time. The Headmaster told governors that his aim was 'to get more co-operation from parents.' He felt that so many boys were 'thoroughly neglected at home.' About 60 parents attended the meeting. Considering the fact that 151 new boys had been admitted this was not a particularly high figure. However it was a very wet night and within two years the numbers attending, what was to become an annual event, had gone up to over 100.

At his first Governors' Meeting in October 1952 Mr Kerrison Jones also made a special plea for an improvement in the condition of the buildings which had not been decorated since the school was opened in 1939. Over the coming year the corridors and then the classrooms were painted in both the Boys' and the Girls' Schools and both Heads expressed their pleasure at the improvement in the learning environment. By the spring of 1954 the Headmaster told governors that he had ordered materials to make a large show case so as to be able to exhibit work made in the handicraft departments. They were also beginning to get a few paintings which, with the freshly painted corridors and rooms, would brighten the school considerably.

The disastrous North Sea floods which occurred on the night of Saturday 31 January 1953 had a major effect on the school since it was designated as a reception centre for people who had to leave their homes. Large areas of King's Lynn were rendered uninhabitable and some 700 people were registered at the school as temporarily homeless. The women and girls were accommodated in the Girls' School buildings and the men and boys in the Boys' School. The school canteen under Mrs Greenacre was in continual use throughout the coming week. The morale of the evacuees was boosted on the Tuesday by a visit from the Queen and Prince Phillip who were still at Sandringham for the Christmas break. They were accompanied by the Duke of Gloucester and various officials. It wasn't until 9 a.m. on the morning of 6 February that all the evacuees had left the school and it did not re-open until Monday 9 February. Attendance on that day was only 64%, no doubt because of the problems local families were still experiencing.

In March 1953 the Headmaster explained to the governors that he planned to report on various aspects of the curriculum from time to time. On this occasion he chose the work done in rural science and gardening which he said gave a very useful training for boys intending to go into agriculture. The department was led by Mr F W Lockley, assisted by Mr J S Waine. In addition there was a technician who also worked half-time as a caretaker. The facilities included a rural-science laboratory, a greenhouse, a potting shed and some 20 acres of garden. The boys grew all varieties of vegetables, fruit and flowers which were sold and the profits were used to buy tools, seeds and fertiliser. There was also a poultry club and eggs were taken each week to the packing station. In addition there were seven bee hives and the boys were trained in bee keeping. It was, Mr Kerrison Jones said, a most successful aspect of the curriculum. Unfortunately the following term he reported that Mr Lockley, who had been at the school since 1945, was retiring and Mr Waine was also leaving. No other reports on aspects of the curriculum have been found.

The pattern of activities during that first year was very much the same as in the past. There were visits to the theatre to see Caryl Jenner productions and to the cinema to see films such as *Ivanhoe, The Pickwick Papers, Henry V* and the film of *The Coronation*. Boys regularly attended the so-called 'lunchtime concerts' now held at the Guildhall, and various speakers came into school to give talks and show films, some of them on career opportunities. Interesting visits later in the school year included a trip to London in March 1953 when 40 boys watched a schoolboy international football match at Wembley Stadium and in the summer term 30 boys went to Fenner's Cricket Ground in Cambridge to see the University Xl play the touring Australian team. In July all the 4th year boys went on a day visit to the Royal Norfolk Show at Narford and on both days of the Show four pupils, accompanied by Mr R Heygate, gave a practical demonstration of their metal-working skills in the Education Tent.

In future years there were trips to Derbyshire, the Royal Tournament at Earls Court, London Airport, the Ford Works at Dagenham, the Norfolk coast and the Broads, the Peakirk Wildfowl Sanctuary and the Perkins Engineering Works in Peterborough and again to Whipsnade Zoo. However in the summer of 1955 the school outing to Oxford had to be cancelled because of a rail strike. Other trips included one to the All-England Boxing Finals in London. Major Gilbert took twelve boys to this event on 12 and 13 April 1954.

During the 1950s the school began to offer boys the chance to travel abroad. The first trip was to Koenigswater in Germany in the 1955 Easter holidays and it was led by Messrs Allen, Fitheridge and Parker. At Whitsun of the same year the Headmaster, Mr Kenyon and Mr Gregory took a group to Jersey. This proved to be a popular destination and there were two trips in 1957, one at Easter and one at Whitsun, both involving some 30 boys, and another in the Whitsun half-term in 1959. Other foreign trips in this period were to Switzerland at Easter in both 1956 and 1957 and to Northern France in 1960 when Mr Christie and Mr Wilson took a group on a cycling tour, to Austria in August 1960 and finally the Headmaster, Mr Macey, Mr Roberts and Mr King took 27 boys to Lucerne in Switzerland in August 1962 on what was described as 'a delightful trip.'

Michael Collinson who was at the school for just one year, 1955-56, and now lives in Australia, remembers the trip to Switzerland:

'We travelled by train across France and stayed at a tiny place called Lauterbrunnen, south of

Interlaken. At the age of twelve I didn't have a Passport, but as we were travelling in a school group we were each issued with an Identity Card signed by the Headmaster F L Kerrison Jones.

We took an exciting rack and pinion train journey inside the Jungfraujock appearing at the top with a view of the snow-covered Eiger Mountain from the lookout where the train stopped. The hotel we were staying at had a wooden sled which three of us borrowed. We had fantastic fun sledging down the hill side below the hotel only to lose control and after falling off watch the sled smash itself into small splinters as it careered into a wood. We had to pay the hotel owner to replace the sled.'

Michael (sixth from the right on the back row of the 1955-56 photograph) also recalls the use of corporal punishment in the school and some of the discipline problems:

'There was corporal punishment at Gaywood Park School which involved an instrument made of three leather thongs called the Taws which was kept in the 'Black Book'. The Mathematics teacher, Mr Beaumont, was always sending boys to fetch the Black Book! He seemed to delight in using the Taws on selected boys.

At the end of one lunch break our music teacher was conducting playground duty and attempting to muster us boys into lines before filing back into class. He instructed one of the boys to come out to the front because he would not stop talking. The boy asked the teacher to take off his glasses and foolishly the teacher did so. The boy promptly struck the teacher full in the face. Needless to say the boy was expelled.'

A 1st year class in 1955-56

A special edition of *The Gaywood Gazette*, produced in 1989 for the 50th anniversary of the opening of the school, has a number of accounts by former pupils. Paul Allen (1959-62) recalls Mr Baldwin's Ford Prefect being lifted up onto some piles of bricks by a group of 4th years and another occasion when some boys taped up the throttle of the groundsman's lawnmower and set it off round the playing field. Both incidents annoyed the staff but were found highly amusing by the pupils. Paul also recalls how strict a teacher was Mr Wisker:

'We held our breath when we went in and did not breathe out until we were well clear of the classroom.'

When asked if he had enjoyed his school days, his reply was, 'Yes, they were fantastic.'

At the end of the summer term 1952 the Lord Lieutenant of Norfolk, Sir Edward Bacon was the guest of honour at the school's Speech Day. The Headmaster would have seen that as quite a coup.

In future years the guest speakers included the Vicar of St Margaret's, the Revd. W Aubrey Aitken, former Headmaster, Dr W Emrys Davies, Mr W O Bell, the Director of the Institute of Education in Cambridge, Colonel John G Glover, the USAF Commandant at Sculthorpe, the Venerable Percival Smith, Archdeacon of Lynn, Mr Lincoln Ralphs, the Chief Education Officer for Norfolk and the Earl of Romney.

During 1953-54 the school had an exchange teacher from America. Mr Henry Shelby from North Andover in Massachusetts temporarily replaced Mr Robert Stevenson on the staff. This was obviously part of a national programme as Mr Shelby was absent from school on 26 October to attend a reception for exchange teachers in London. He had also been absent for two days the previous week to meet his fiancée who was arriving in Southampton from New York. They were married at Our Lady's Roman Catholic Church on London Road at the end of October. The following month both Mr and Mrs Shelby took part in an Anglo-American Brains Trust in the school hall which was attended by parents and friends. Miss Winnifred Dore, the Headmistress of the Girls' High School, and two education officers were also on the panel.

Most of the annual events which had taken place in the past continued during Mr Kerrison Jones's headship. One that has not been mentioned previously was an annual bring-and-buy sale on one afternoon in the autumn term when the school was closed to allow it to take place. The first mention of a bring-and-buy sale was in October 1950 when the aim was to raise money for the Guildhall Restoration Fund. However later sales were held in aid of school funds. In October 1952 over £100 was raised and the following year £96. In some years part of the money raised was donated to charity, for example, in 1959 £75 was sent to the Norfolk branch of the World Refugee Fund and in 1962, of the £93 raised, £45 'was donated to charities concerned with children.'

On the sporting front inter-house competitions continued with football and boxing in the autumn term, football and cross-country running in the spring term, and athletics, cricket and swimming in the summer term. The photographs show the successful house athletics and cricket teams in 1956.

Vancouver House athletics team in 1956

The successful house cricket team in 1956

One rather unusual order of events was that the school swimming gala was always held at the very end of the summer term and after the King's Lynn Schools' and the Norfolk Schools' galas. It is unclear therefore how entries for the local competition were decided upon. The photograph - provided by John Fysh, who is third from the left on the back row - shows the school swimming team which took part in the County Gala in 1958.

The school was often successful in the King's Lynn Secondary Schools' Sports and sometimes sent athletes to the County and even the National finals. In 1952 Terry Chapman's javelin throw of 135 feet 2 inches in the U17 group beat the previous record by 3 feet 5 inches in the County Final but was not long enough to send him to the All-England Championships at Bradford. The following year Walter Hewitt in the 13-15 age group threw 128 feet 4 inches at the County Final, breaking the previous record by 10 feet 2 inches. In the summer of 1954 Graham Thomson was selected to represent Norfolk in the hurdles at the National Sports in Ashington. He was clearly an all-round sportsman as he had also been awarded County Colours for football. At the Speech Day in July 1954 Graham was awarded a Silver Medal for PE by the guest speaker the Revd. W A Aitken, Vicar of St. Margaret's Church. However it was not Graham but A Medlock who had been joint winner of the Alderman Allen Cup for outstanding performance at the King's Lynn Sports on 16 June 1954. There was a major success in 1957 when J Ely stayed on at school an extra term in order to compete in the All-England Sports at Southampton. It was well worth it as he won the intermediate pole-vault competition with a leap of 10 feet 6 inches against the best schoolboy opposition in the country. The previous year, at Plymouth, Norfolk had won the minor counties championship but on this occasion they were in third place.

The school swimming team in 1958

The King's Lynn Sports Day was usually held on the Gaywood Park playing fields, although in June 1959 it was held at Alderman Catleugh School. That year the star performer for the Boys' School was Colin Clarke who cleared 9 feet 3 inches in the pole vault and was joint holder, together with Chris Kerry from K.E.S., of the Alderman Allen Cup. H Collison came 1st and J Edwards 3rd in the hop, skip and jump and B Rudd set a new record in the 11-13 javelin with a throw of 113 feet 10 inches. The previous summer Colin Williamson was awarded the Alderman Allen Cup for the outstanding performance in the 13-15 age group. His pole vault height of 9 feet equalled the national standard.

Relatively little information on inter-school football or cricket in this period has been found. However on 9 April 1954 the school beat Fakenham 1-0 and won the Secondary Schools' Football Shield. It was presented by former Deputy Head, Mr Oliver Davison. The 1955-56 season was also said to be a very successful one. Of the five or six teams regularly playing on a Saturday it was 'rare for more than one of them to be beaten.' Photographs of junior football teams from the mid-1950s are included. The member of staff is Mr Jimmy Lupson who left to join Alderman Catleugh Boys' School in 1957. Occasionally there were matches against teams from the American base at Sculthorpe, for example in April 1957 and again in December later that year. In 1960-61 the 1st Xl and the U13 teams were involved in the Football Shield matches at the Grammar School and the school won the Lynn Junior Shield. As in other periods Gaywood boys were successful in becoming professional footballers. Graham Reed left Lynn in 1954 to join Sunderland and his school pal, Graham Thomson, shortly afterwards was signed by Tottenham Hotspur.

An exciting sporting opportunity took place in November 1961 when 40 boys went to a special coaching session at the Grammar School led by Billy Wright who had played for Wolverhampton

Mr Lupson and a junior football team in 1955-56. *Back row: Peter Langford; John Neal; Barry Lilley; Eddie Addicott; Andy Bone; Michael Bray; Donald Daw; Peter Goldsmith.*
Front row: Colin Clarke; Lewis Donald; Gordon Bowring (Captain); John Fysh; Keith Branham.

1956-57 Junior football team. *Back row: Colin Clarke; Eddie Addicott; Sonny Yallop; Barry Lilley; Peter Farmer; John Fysh; Andy Bone. Front row: Roger Oliver; Arty Hunter; Colin Parlett; Gordon Bowring (Captain); Dougie Empson; Donald Daw; Peter Goldsmith.*

Wanderers and England in the 1940s and 1950s. He was made England Captain in 1948 and in all made 105 appearances for his country.

Boxing had been included in the inter-house competitions since 1944 and from 1947 the finals had been held on one evening before Christmas to allow parents to attend. In the spring of 1956, following the Norfolk Schoolboys' Boxing Tournament, six Gaywood Park pupils were selected to box for Norfolk. The school had even greater success the following year when some twenty boys took part in the County Finals, which were held at Gaywood Park. Twelve were selected to box for Norfolk against Suffolk at Diss and seven were chosen to represent the Eastern Counties in London. There was similar success in future years.

One new annual sporting event, which was introduced in March 1956, was a gymnastics display put on in an evening for parents and friends of the school. Also during this period two new sports were offered to the boys – fencing and basketball. In June 1960 it was reported by that the newly formed basketball team had competed with considerable success in a tournament at Thorpe in Norwich.

The Cadet Force, under Captain Gaukroger, was still active in the 1950s and early 1960s. In the summer of 1961 the unit won a Challenge Cup for .303 rifle shooting when it represented Norfolk against teams from Cambridgeshire, Suffolk and Essex.

Another inter-school competition in which Gaywood Park boys took part for a few years was the annual Civics Quiz organised by the National Association of Local Government Officers (NALGO). The school team lost in the first round to Wells in 1960 but the following year having beaten a

The Army Cadet Corps in the mid 1950s. Back row: Paul Chase; Ray Osbourne; Trevor Fountain; Barry Wilson. Front row: Mick Collison; Captain Gaukroger; Gerry Foreman.

team from Wells lost to Swaffham in the second round. No information on what happened in 1962 has been found but in 1963 the school team was knocked out in the first round by Fakenham.

Music and drama productions tended to be at the end of the autumn term. Some years there were end-of-term concerts as in 1952, 1958, 1959, 1961 and 1962; in others there was a school play. In December 1953, for example, this was *Toad of Toad Hall* by A A Milne, dress rehearsals of which were seen by the boys during school time and then there were public performances on two evenings. It was said that this production by Mr Nelson was of a very high standard. Unfortunately he was to leave in the summer of 1954 having been appointed Deputy Head of a new school in Aylesbury. The following year the school drama society put on three one-act plays; in December 1955 *Treasure Island* was the school production; and in 1956 it was *High Explosive*. The only other mention found of a school play was of one at the end of the spring term 1960 when there was a production of *The Ghost Train* by Arnold Ridley. However, as in the summer of 1952 mentioned above, Gaywood Park pupils also got involved in drama outside school. In June 1954, for example, 24 boys and the same number of girls performed a country dance in an episode depicting the visit of Henry Vll to King's Lynn as part of the town's Charter Week celebrations. There were public performances on four evenings.

Michael Collinson, cited above, was in the *Treasure Island* production in 1955:

> 'The school put on a play for the parents, Treasure Island. The cast had real swords, flint lock guns and pistols. I don't know how they managed that. The firearm regulations must have been quite different back in 1956. I was one of Squire Trelawney's men fighting against Long John Silver and his pirates. I had just one line in the play, "I think so sir," I stated in response to the question "Did you get him?" after I had fired my musket at a pirate over the stockade fence.'

A carol service was held every year. For two years it took place jointly with the Girls' School: in December 1954 it was at St Margaret's Church; and the following year at St Nicholas Chapel. However in future years the two schools held separate services because of the problem of numbers. The Boys' School regularly took part in the King's Lynn Musical Festival and in the School Choirs' Festival at the Albert Hall in London. When Mr Allen took some boys and girls to London in the summer of 1959 the Headmaster reported to the governors that they 'were the only schools from Norfolk represented at that event'. Some opportunities were offered to boys to learn musical instruments, for example in September 1960 Mr Bassett started violin lessons with a 'small but keen group' of six boys. However no further references to the school brass band formed in October 1949 have been found.

Cultural opportunities offered to the boys during Mr Kerrison Jones's first year are mentioned above. In future years there were annual visits by groups to the Caryl Jenner plays at the Guildhall and to other productions such as that by the Plantagenet Players of *Macbeth* in February 1954 seen by 160 boys. Visits to the Guildhall to attend concerts also continued, albeit less frequently than in the past.

Occasionally the school was taken to see films. The whole school saw *The Conquest of Everest* at the Majestic Cinema in January 1954, 140 boys went to the Guildhall in April 1956 to see *Christopher Columbus* and the whole school saw *Richard lll* at the Majestic the following month. Sometimes films were shown in school. Often these were on careers or educational films made by companies such as Cadburys or Brooke Bond but sometimes they were of more general interest such as the film of the 1960 Olympic Games in Rome. At the end of the spring term 1963 the whole school watched *The Trial and Crucifixion of Jesus.*

Staff turnover was quite high in this period, including two changes of Deputy Head. Mr R J Auchterlonie left at the end of the summer term 1954 to be Head of the new St Edmund's Junior School in North Lynn and was replaced by Mr H S Kenyon. He stayed only until Christmas 1957, having been appointed Headmaster at Terrington Secondary Modern School, and was succeeded by Mr R O Powell as from Easter 1958. Instability of staffing was one of the problems identified in an HMI Report based on a full inspection which took place between 31 January and 3 February 1955. It highlighted the fact that the Headmaster was the fourth to be in post since 1939 and that of the 25 assistant teachers twelve had come into the school since his own appointment in 1952 and seven had joined the staff in the autumn of 1954. The report pointed out that the Headmaster had initially faced difficulties because of his inexperience of schools of this type. However he had 'shown qualities of kindliness and quick perception, together with administrative ability' and there was 'good reason to believe' that the school would 'prosper under his direction.' It was also said that the Deputy Head, Mr Kenyon, was 'a well-qualified and able master' whose teaching was 'strong and effective' and that the 'support and help' he had given the Headmaster had 'proved invaluable.' Unfortunately, as mentioned above, he did not stay much longer at Gaywood Park.

At the time of the inspection there were 602 boys on roll. The annual intake was approximately 150, including some 10 to 15 boys from reorganised village schools and a special intake of 40 to 50 boys at 14 plus from un-reorganised schools. The boys were divided into 18 forms: five in Year 1; five in Year 2; four in Year 3; and four in Year 4. Except in the 4th Year the classes were streamed by ability. In order to keep the size down in the remedial forms – there were 17 in 1E, 22 in 2E and 34 in 3D - the numbers in the others were very high. Nine forms had more than 35 pupils and of those three were above 40. The 4th Year curriculum had changed since the previous inspection in 1948. There was an academic course (4A), two parallel technical courses (4T1 and 4T2), one

Mr D Macey and his class in about 1953

biased towards engineering and the other towards building, and an agriculture course (4Ag.)

The report said that there was excellent co-operation with the Youth Employment Service and the majority of boys found no difficulty in finding work on leaving school. About 10% went on to further education at the King's Lynn Technical College.

By 1955 as well as the main block there was a prefabricated building containing two workshops and two classrooms. In all there were 22 teaching spaces. Some suggestions were made on how the teaching spaces might be improved but the main criticism was that the library was also used as a classroom. The book stock of 1000 fiction and 500 non-fiction was also totally insufficient. At least 1000 more books were needed to meet minimum requirements.

A class group in about 1956

The report was also critical about the dining facilities. The kitchen-dining room was shared with the Girls' School and had been built to serve 350 to 400 meals each day. By 1955 it was serving upwards of 650. Some three or more classrooms in each school had to be used for dining as well as there being two sittings in the dining room. The solution suggested was the provision of an additional kitchen-dining room so that each school had its own facility.

The report was complimentary about the school as a community:

'The School has passed beyond the stage of purely authoritative control and as a result of successful training by the staff the boys have now achieved a creditable measure of self-discipline. Prefects and house captains are taking ever-increasing responsibility for routine matters in the general conduct of the school. The boys are friendly and responsive; the majority are taking increasing pride in their appearance and deeper interest in the general life of the school. As a social community the School is, as yet, relatively undeveloped but the wholesome relationship that is springing up between the Masters and the boys augurs well for the future....Voluntary clubs and societies, which cover a wide range of interests, are developing on good lines. The School programme of outside visits is full and varied. There is close co-operation with Governors and parents and the School's open days and other functions are well supported….The School maintains a company of the Army Cadet Force.'

In the section on curriculum and standards of work the report was also complimentary:

'The Headmaster must be commended on the sound aims which he has formulated for his School and on his conception of a curriculum and organisation in which an appropriate balance is held between academic and practical subjects and between general and specialist teaching. It is evident that careful thought has been given to the comprehensive schemes of work in which due provision is made for differentiation between the streams.'

The report said that with 25 assistant teachers there was 'naturally considerable variation in the quality and effectiveness of the teaching' but there was 'a praiseworthy general level of competence.' Where there was a lack of success it was 'due mainly to the lack of experience and to the unformed

Mr Allen and the Prefects in about 1956

standards of the Masters concerned and not to any lack of enthusiasm or industry.' Particular mention was made of 'the high standard of workmanship in the practical subjects' and the degree of success achieved in the teaching of religious instruction. Detailed comments were made on the teaching of each subject and helpful suggestions as to how improvements could be achieved were made. In general it was felt that teaching was most successful if it was in the hands of a few teachers with one having overall responsibility for a subject. The fact that English was taught by the form masters with the aim of giving as many of the staff as possible responsibility for such a fundamental subject was not seen as 'an unqualified success' and ought to be reconsidered.

The report's conclusion was as follows:

'In view of the fact that the school has suffered from abnormal staff changes its general progress, particularly during the past year, is commendable. The bearing of the boys has improved and there are many signs of increased self-respect and of a more wholesome attitude towards work. Good social relationships between staff and pupils are being developed and a sense of community is being fostered.

Achievement in several fields is encouraging and it is to be hoped that a steady advance in the all-round quality of the work will follow.'

At least one recommendation in the HMI report was acted upon, albeit after some considerable delay. In the spring term of 1960 discussions took place on the building of a new canteen. It was finally opened a year later in January 1961 some six years after HMI had suggested that the need for such a building was urgent. For the first time in many years no classrooms in either school had to be used as dining spaces.

In July 1962, having been at the school for ten years, the Headmaster reported to the governors on the progress made during his time in post. He said that the lack of qualified and experienced staff had been the main problem he had faced. To give an example from an earlier report, in the three years from 1958 to 1961 only two permanent posts had been filled by qualified teachers; there had been 13 temporary appointments and eight of them were of unqualified staff. Other examples have already been cited above. He was pleased to report that the boys were of 'a better type than they were some years ago when there were in the school quite a large number of boys of a rough and undesirable type. The boys of the school at present are, on the whole, well behaved, friendly and anxious to do well.' He also felt that the parents were more interested in the future of their children than in the past.

As well as staff leaving for promotion or to widen their experience, 1962 saw the retirement of one of the original 1939 staff. Mr Lewis Turner was off ill for most of the autumn term 1961 and he retired at the end of the following January. One of his pupils, John Bocking (1941-44), more than 50 years after leaving school, described him as a 'very talented teacher of woodwork'.

Mr Kerrison Jones retired at the end of the spring term 1963 having been ill for some considerable time. He was admitted to Addenbrooke's Hospital in Cambridge in June 1961 for an operation and again in January 1963. Mr Powell was Acting Headmaster for two long periods, firstly in the second half of the summer term 1961 and secondly for the whole of the spring term 1963; Mr A G Skerritt stepped up to act as Deputy during these periods. Between the Headmaster's two long periods of absence Mr Powell was himself off ill for two months with rheumatic fever.

Fortunately the Headmaster was well enough to attend, with his wife, the final assembly of the spring term on 9 April 1963 when he was presented with a number of leaving gifts. Richard Page in 3B presented a silver tea service on behalf of the boys, Malcolm Lovick, the Head Boy, a set of cut-glass wine glasses on behalf of the prefects, and Mr Percy Wisker, an armchair on behalf of the staff. Unfortunately Mr Kerrison Jones did not long survive his retirement. His death was reported in the press on 24 July 1964.

5. A force for change at the Boys' School, 1963 to 1970

After the resignation of Mr Kerrison Jones, the headship of the Boys School was advertised. There were 46 applicants for the post and from a long list of twenty-two six were selected for interview on 30 January 1963. One person withdrew his application and so five were actually interviewed. The post was offered to Mr George A Fell as from the start of the summer term 1963. He had previously taught at Upwell and Downham Market Secondary Schools.

Mr G A Fell

Mr Fell was a much more forceful personality than his predecessor. According to Mr John Youngman, who was on the staff from 1965 to 1997, he managed to ruffle the feathers of many of the older guard because he was quite critical of the way the school operated. However he was able to inspire confidence in the younger members of staff. He certainly introduced a much tougher disciplinary regime into the school.

At his first Governors' Meeting in June he presented a two-page special report in which he listed the inadequacies, as he saw them, of the school premises which he said were not in many respects suitable for a school in the 1960s. The toilets were unheated and unhygienic; there were no separate washing basins, rather a long trough with cold taps at intervals; and the urinals were stained and unpleasant. In addition the grounds were very untidy. He suggested that the derelict cadet hut and rifle range should be removed; he did not see the army cadet unit as something he would want to continue, except as an out-of-school activity. He also suggested various improvements to the teaching accommodation for science, rural studies and craft, and he said that the appointment of both a workshop assistant and a laboratory assistant was necessary to facilitate the smooth running of the craft and science departments. He also proposed that there should be a Head of English in addition to the Heads of Heavy Craft and PE, since English was a vital subject in the curriculum and in any case there were far more English periods taught than either craft or PE. A final plea was for new blackboards, which he said should be fixed to the walls rather than hanging in front of cupboards, and for new audio equipment.

New head teachers have a distinct advantage in getting changes implemented. At that first Governors' Meeting it was resolved that the Territorial Army would be asked to remove the cadet hut and rifle range, and that the derelict greenhouse and potting shed should also be removed. Plans and estimates for a new potting shed, greenhouse and gardening room, the re-organisation of the craft rooms and the removal of cupboards and a supply of new blackboards were to be requested.

It would however take some time for many of the changes asked for by the Headmaster to be put into effect. In November Mr Fell told the governors that he was very pleased with the new VHF radio, record player and tape recorder which had been provided. New octagonal dining tables - not mentioned in the report referred to above - had also been supplied to enable a change to 'family service' whereby the staff and pupils ate together. The Headmaster said that he believed this 'to be an excellent addition to school life.' By February 1964 the old cadet hut had been removed and a brick-built hut previously used by the cadets was being fitted out as a room for rural studies. A new Head of English, Mr K G David, was appointed as from the first of March 1964. A technician shared between craft and science was also appointed and by the summer of 1965 a second was requested by the Headmaster and this was supported by the governors. However it was not until June 1967 that it was reported that the LEA had accepted a tender of £8019.6s.1d. for the requested improvements to the art, science and craft rooms and that the work had begun.

Mr Fell had a number of other changes he intended to introduce. In November 1963 he announced that homework was to be given to all boys as he wanted to be ready to enter candidates for the new secondary school examinations due to be introduced in 1965. By June the following year he was able to report that 'almost without exception' every boy in the 'A' stream did homework each night, about nine out of ten in the 'B' stream, half the boys in the 'C' stream and about a third of those in the 'D' stream. In the summer of 1964 19 boys were entered for the Royal Society of Arts (RSA) examinations in arithmetic, mathematics and English Language. This was the first time any boys from the school had been entered for an external examination. In future years, in addition to RSA examinations, boys were entered for the General Certificate of Education (GCE) and the Certificate of Secondary Examination (CSE). In the 1966 summer examinations eight out of eleven boys entered were successful in gaining some GCE passes and in the spring of 1967 Mr Fell told governors that the school could now offer a full range of subjects at GCE 'O' level. Numbers staying on at school for a fifth year and taking external examinations increased each year. In 1967 15 boys passed 'O' level examinations, four of them - Haydn Forster, Allan Frost, Paul Gray and Raymond Solly - in five subjects, 11 got CSE passes and 53 were successful in gaining RSA certificates. Andrew Moore, although only 16 years old, successfully passed at 'A' level in British Constitution, as well as three 'O' levels and one CSE. In the RSA examinations Luis Jorba gained a distinction in mathematics with a score of 92%. The following year two boys got 'A' level passes in British Constitution, 13 out of the 22 boys entered passed in at least one subject at 'O' level, and only 14 boys out of 69 failed to get an RSA certificate.

In both 1965 and 1968 newspaper articles examine the changes which Mr Fell had introduced into the school. In the first of these headed 'Revolutionary Methods at Gaywood Park Boys' School' (*Lynn News*, 8 June 1965), the Headmaster's philosophy is set out clearly. For example he was unhappy with rigid streaming of pupils so in the first two years it had been replaced by groups devised virtually at random, although care was taken to break up any cliques that might have developed and there were still special facilities to help those who were struggling with reading. In the fourth year the classes were either geared to public examinations or to more practical courses. There was much work done to provide careers guidance through talks and visits and civics courses provided preparation for life after school.

Also in 1965 it was decided to change the labelling of year groups and forms. The first year became A, the second year B, the third year C and so on. John Youngman says that this was a result of a suggestion he made to Mr Fell who wanted to make it less obvious to pupils that they were in low ability groups.

Another article, this time in the *Eastern Daily Press* (6 February 1968), was headed 'The Quiet Revolution at Lynn School.' The success of pupils in public examinations is described and one of the boys mentioned above, Allan Frost, by this time taking three 'A' levels, is quoted as saying that 'it is a free and easy atmosphere which really encourages you….The teachers are so willing to help on every occasion. You are treated like young men, not like a boy who has to be told what to do all the time.' Mr Fell was said to be 'bubbling over with ideas.'

As in previous years staffing changes were an annual or even more frequent event. One of the original 1939 staff, art teacher Mr James Beckett, retired at the end of the summer term 1963. The Deputy Head, Mr R O Powell, who had been Acting Head for two long spells in 1961 and 1963, was appointed to a headship at Market Rasen Secondary School in Lincolnshire as from January 1964. His successor, Mr R E Gent from West Winch, took up his post after Easter. One of the longest serving teachers, Mr Harold Allen, who had joined the staff in October 1940, died on 21 May 1964. September 1965 saw the retirement of Mr Eric Allsop who had been at the school nearly twenty years as a teacher of rural studies. Mr Fell said that he had given 'excellent service and was worthy of commendation.'

Two other long-serving teachers were shortly to retire: Mr Percy Wisker in July 1966; and Mr Arthur Skerritt at Christmas 1966. The latter had on several occasions been Acting Deputy Head and Mr Fell said that 'he had served both this school and Norfolk Education Committee well and loyally. I personally shall miss both his skill as a teacher and his advice as a wise and mature educationalist.' Another very valuable member of staff left at Easter 1969. The Deputy Head, Mr Ron Gent, had been appointed Assistant Warden at Soham Village College where he was to be in charge of the Secondary Modern School. Mr Fell told the governors that 'the school will greatly miss him. He has done a thoroughly good job of work at this school and is worthy of high praise.' His successor was Mr T D Norman. The last of the long-serving staff to retire in this period was Mr Ernest Fitheridge who had been at the school since 1947. He left at Easter 1970. There were of course many other changes of teaching and non-teaching staff.

Each year boys took part in number of school trips, some related to potential employment opportunities or at any rate of a vocational nature, for example to the King's Lynn Docks, the Fire Station, the Sugar Beet Factory, Campbell's Soups, Miller's Turkey Farm at Great Massingham, the Terrington Research Station, the Metal Box Factory in Wisbech, Great Yarmouth Power Station, Pye Electricals at Cambridge, Perkins Engines in Peterborough, the Triumph Motor Company in Coventry, the GPO Sorting Office in Norwich, Sizewell Power Station, the Port of London, the Ford Works at Dagenham and Vauxhall Motors in Luton. Other visits were of more general educational interest such as those to St Margaret's Church, Ely Cathedral, Coventry Cathedral, the King's Lynn Museum, Norwich Museum, the Royal Norfolk Show, the House of Commons, the National and Tate Galleries, Castle Rising and Grime's Graves near Thetford. Many more examples could be cited.

The tradition of taking boys on foreign holidays continued but with no regularity. The Headmaster led his first such trip at Whitsun 1964 to Germany. The group travelled through the Rhine Gorge and visited Cologne and Bonn. Mr Fell's somewhat lukewarm statement was that it was 'a success from most standpoints.' Boys were also taken on the educational cruises sponsored by Norfolk County Education Committee, for example nine boys and one teacher joined the *Dunera* for a Mediterranean cruise in October 1963. The only other reference found was to another cruise from 28 February to 15 March 1968 which took in Spain, Italy, Greece and Turkey but the numbers involved were not given.

The Headmaster decided to re-introduce open days for parents. In December 1963 there was an exhibition of art, sculpture, pottery, craft, drama and PE which was attended by upwards of 600 people. He intended that this would be repeated in the summer term and become a regular event but other details have not been found.

A school magazine was not produced regularly at the Boys' School, but in 1965 one was brought out covering the school year 1964-65, perhaps to commemorate the twenty-five years since the school was opened. Certainly there was a long and reflective article by Percy Wisker, on the teaching staff since 1939, which is reproduced below:

'In September 1939 Gaywood Park School opened its doors to admit all boys over the age of eleven who had previously attended other schools in the town. These schools now closed or were made available for primary pupils. As war had been declared the boys were sent home for a week while staff were employed in finding temporary homes for children evacuated from London. While boys did not object to this unexpected extension of their summer holiday they were not so sure that they wanted to leave the schools that they knew for the school with which they were not familiar. One boy was unwise enough to say he liked his old school better because he had done no work there. In spite of the worries of wartime the school carried on quietly with its activities, even though the staff became fewer and fewer as younger members joined the Forces, and the boys became more numerous as more children came to live in the town. A London school shared our buildings.

After the war Gaywood Park School underwent considerable change. The staff began to grow as men returned from war service, and the number of boys in the school rose sharply because pupils from schools in surrounding villages travelled by bus to attend, and later the school leaving age was raised to fifteen years. The school was bursting at the seams, and a solution was found by building a new school to which village boys could go, keeping Gaywood Park for town residents.

The progress of the school has, of course, been the story of the pupils and their achievements have been so varied that it is difficult to do more than give a few examples of what has occurred in twenty-six years. The record in most sporting activities is very good indeed. Boys have represented the school, town and county in football, cricket, athletics, boxing, swimming, basketball and shooting and they have competed in national championships throughout England.

The first aim of the school has been to fit boys to live happy lives in the adult world. Hundreds of boys are in interesting and responsible positions in industry and trade and every year more boys join their ranks.

However large the school buildings may be, and however extensive its playing fields, the school itself is made of a very big group of boys, and in writing of boys each one can provide a story. On one wall of the school hall, for example, is a brass plate which pays tribute to the scholar who lost his life in saving his brother from drowning. It is possible to go on writing of boys who were outstanding while at school; others who quietly and modestly plodded on each day; some who by cheerfulness and a sense of fun made the years enjoyable; those who achieved very little it seemed at the time but succeeded after schooldays were over.

Now, many, of them have sons here, all looking forward. They may appear different from those who went before, their masters may teach in a different way, their lessons may take a different form, but this generation of boys will add one more chapter to the school story.

What is written here is only a glimpse of the school, with its excitements, its dullness, its fun and its tears, its hopes and disappointments. The story will be told again but the actors who bring it to life will be changed.'

The 1965 Magazine gives a snapshot of the school in the middle of the 1960s. It highlights the school's success in sport over the previous year. The 1st Xl Football Team was said to have been the best since 1951-52, having won 20, drawn 2 and lost only 6 out of its 28 matches under the captaincy of D Benefer. In Basketball the Senior Team had won 7 out of its 9 matches and R Woodhouse and P Johnson had played in the County Team, the former as its Captain. The school was less successful in cricket having been knocked out of the county competition in the first round. Nevertheless the 1st Xl won 5 out of its 8 matches during the season.

There was also information about non-sporting activities. The School Choir had performed on two occasions, the first as part of the massed choirs in the King's Lynn Festival production of *Noye's Fludde* with three boys taking solo parts - Peter Rye, Ian Frost and Owen Sedgewick. At Speech Day the choir sang four songs and the Thomas Tallis *Canon*. It was also reported that a Chess and Draughts Club had been formed in 1964, meeting at lunchtimes in the autumn and spring terms. The membership had topped 80.

In the summer of 1965 some 55 boys were entered for the Royal Society of Arts CSE examinations and three of them, Murray Cleaver, Peter Gamble and Andrew Moore gained group certificates, having passed in five subjects including English Language. Two boys gained G.S.E. certificates: Brian Frost in English Language and British Constitution; and Richard Hitchcock in British Constitution.

Perhaps the most interesting piece in the whole magazine was a letter from G O Towler who had been at the school from 1954-58:

> 'I thought that you and some of the staff....would like to know that I have just obtained a 1st Class B.Sc. Special Honours degree in physics at Queen Mary College, London. In October I will be going to Imperial College, London, to do research for my Ph.D. At the moment I am having a good time at C.E.R.N. in Switzerland, helping with data analysis.
>
> I would like to thank your staff, and the staff at the Technical College, for all the help they gave me in getting to university.'

Mr Fell and his Prefects in the mid 1960s

Mr Towler was by no means the only person who had failed his 11-plus examination and went to Gaywood Park but was later to be successful in gaining a university or equivalent professional qualification. It was an invidious system in which some 25% of pupils were misplaced in either grammar or secondary modern schools at age 11. One very successful former pupil is local historian Dr Paul Richards (1956-60) who also took GSEs and 'A' levels at the Technical College before going to Birmingham University where he gained both his first degree and then his Ph.D. He also has a Post-graduate Certificate in Education from Nottingham University. Paul is a former Mayor of Lynn, an Honorary Alderman, the only Honorary Borough Freeman, a Deputy Lieutenant of Norfolk and the author of several books on the local area. Quite a curriculum vitae for someone who was failed by the 11-plus system.

Another ex-Gaywood pupil who was to become a well-known solicitor in King's Lynn is Colin Bailey (1964-69). Having taken 'A' levels at the Technical College he went on to Leicester University where he gained a degree in Law. He cites not only his own case but that of the twins, Richard and Tony Mobbs, to demonstrate the unfairness of 11-plus selection. Richard went to Gaywood Park with Colin but Tony passed the entry examination and went to the Grammar School. While Richard took his 'A' levels at the College, Tony did his at K.E.S. However they both were accepted for science degrees at Leicester University and eventually became lecturers there.

Colin Bailey has written a detailed account of his time at the school some of which is reproduced below:

'I had failed the 11 plus and had been told as a failure I would now have to attend Gaywood Park Secondary Boys' School which had the reputation of being the most violent school within the region. Luckily for me my attendance coincided with the appointment of two major influences on my life, Mr Fell, the Head Master of Gaywood, and Mr Gent, the Deputy Head.

My first memory of attending the school was being called to the main hall to witness both Mr Fell and Mr Gent striding across the raised stage whilst all the boys sat in complete awe of this man who threatened to thrash anybody who misbehaved but would reward those that worked hard. With cane in hand Mr Fell was an imposing figure who had apparently been sent to the school to bring some order to chaos.

At that time if you were "sentenced" to Gaywood Park you had no opportunity to take O levels; if you wanted to proceed to further education you would have to go to the local technical college where you would be at least a year behind your counterparts from the grammar school as they deemed it inappropriate for you to sit O levels until you had spent two years at the technical college. Mr Fell believed that was completely wrong and that pupils at Gaywood Park were capable of achieving exams results equal to those at the grammar school....Mr Fell believed that we were capable of more than simply rotavating the garden at Gaywood Park which previous pupils had been assigned to....

The staff however at that time were dedicated to those who showed an inclination to work. In particular people like John Wooll who took English, Mr Fell who made me believe I could study economics and Mr Gent who took history, as well as Mr Macey who encouraged me in geography and made me believe that I could go on to sit A levels and ultimately attend university, something which at the age of eleven I certainly believed I would not be able to do.

Many of the other pupils at Gaywood Park benefited from the new regime and I can remember Steven Valentine, who was a year older than me, also attended university and who finished his working life as a headmaster in a very large comprehensive school in Keighley, Yorkshire. Other colleagues ended up as professional footballers as Gaywood was always a very sporting school.

I look back on my attendance at Gaywood and it probably encouraged me to work harder than I would have done if I had attended the grammar school; it certainly made me aware of what I could achieve if I worked hard but is also reminded me that the system, as it was then, allowed many pupils to fall between the cracks never to reappear again.'

Steve Valentine, mentioned in Colin Bailey's piece above, was at the school from 1962 to 1966. He too has written at length about his time at the school and some of his memories are very evocative, for example about the teachers:

'They were frightening, especially to a small 11-year old boy…. the 'old guard' male staff most of whom had seen service in the Second World War….were battle hardened. A school of testosterone teenage boys would not strike fear in their hearts having faced 'Jerry' on the other end of a bayonet or survived the Arctic waters and the torpedoes on their way to Murmansk. Most loved their subject, and were keen to impart their knowledge. They gave their time freely to the boys who wanted to learn with after school sessions….each ran some games team after school irrespective of….sporting acumen or not. It was 'chalk and talk' teaching…. The younger staff, straight out of college, were a shock to the boys' system as they were so different to the 'old guard'. They were fresh and enthusiastic and took an interest in you – not too sure many of us were too keen on being taken 'an interest in'; we just wanted to be left alone and allowed to get on with it.'

His recollection of links with the Girls' School will strike a cord with many who went to single-sex schools:

'The girls' school was right next to the boys', separated by a path and patrolled by staff. Definitely, no fraternising. You had contact with the girls just once in your school career, at the school dance, held when you were in the 4th Year of your schooling….We practiced proper dancing in the hall during the weeks leading to the event with some boys taking the lead and with others taking the girl's role. Psychologically quite scarring. I'm sure there are some former pupils out there who still haven't got over the experience. Even more damaging was when the event finally arrived, totally alcohol free and highly chaperoned, successfully executed by the staff, some of whom must have been prisoners of war at some time and knew all the tricks in the book. Having learnt how to dance as a girl does not bode well when you actually dance with one. Holding a girl was a novel experience and there was much lusting going on that night but not much else. How this prepared us to live in a world where there are girls passed me by.'

Steve stresses the importance of sport at the school in the 1960s and also the importance of being good at it to have kudos among one's peers:

'The school was divided up into houses….We competed against each other in every sport imaginable after school in all weathers – drought, flood and pestilence never stopped a game. Through hail, snow and gales the matches always took place. Competition was fierce and no prisoners were taken….The greatest uncivilised event, held on a nice frosty February day, was the whole-school house cross-country race. Malingerers were not allowed, everyone had to take part. A note from your parents would be ripped up and a doctor's note treated with equal contempt and scorn. A broken leg or consigned to a wheelchair might, I say might, demote you to being a marshal…. Your finishing position mattered, another example of 'know thy place' in society. Coming in 151st in your year counted towards the house total and was therefore important. There was an incentive not to come in last in your house or year group as this meant that you wouldn't be beaten up behind the bike sheds after the competition. Sports winners were heralded as heroes and lauded by all, losers were shirked and derided – it seemed, at the time, a proper preparation for life.'

I was also much amused by Steve's description of school meals:

'The school meals were very much a reflection of the times. A new system of family tables of eight had been introduced - 2 boys from each year if I recall correctly. The youngest, the slave, went to collect the meal for the table. The oldest boy served everyone else. As a result – lion pride feeding. The oldest got all the best bits of the meal, that is the meat, and the youngest got the cabbage that no one wanted that had been on the stove since eight o'clock that morning. Semolina and jam was always a favourite, the 1st formers not getting it until they were in their last year. Staff did question the unequal distribution of food....to be told the younger pupils didn't like what the older boys were tucking into, only to be confirmed vigorously by the starving juniors.'

I shall quote just one more section from Steve Valentine's contribution and it concerns discipline and punishment:

'Schools in the1960's were brutal institutions. The staff....used physical punishment as a means of keeping control of potentially unruly children. The use of the slipper, the ruler across unsuspecting knuckles, the flying pieces of chalk and even board rubbers were endemic and not controlled or applied with any rationale. Being caned by the Headmaster....was a weekly occurrence. I was caned in public, in assembly twice....[On one of the occasions] I was caught on the Thursday and the public flogging always took place on the stage on Friday morning. So I had all Thursday night to worry about it and to plan. The next morning I went to school prepared for my 'six of the best'. I was wearing two pairs of swimming trunks plus extra pants. It would hurt but not as much! I was called up by the Headmaster and bent over to be caned on the bottom BUT I had been rumbled. I was told to stand up and put my hand out....'

However Steve Valentine concludes that 'Gaywood was a good school which provided excellent opportunities for a whole range of boys.' He said that it was the platform which allowed him to go on to have a university education and a successful career in teaching – 'not bad for an 11-year old failure.'

Nick Fisher (1963-67) also has happy memories of the school despite the fact that he was not good at sport. One of his favourite teachers was Larry Seaman who taught him for games and also geography and was his form teacher in his last year. 'He was a good teacher, firm but fair and would talk to you not at you. You knew exactly where you stood with him.' The Headmaster, Mr Fell, was 'a strict authoritarian with a booming voice' and in Nick's opinion he 'was very good at his job.' Another teacher who impressed Nick was Mrs Morrison who taught him art. She 'was absolutely brilliant. It didn't matter how good or bad you were at art - I was rubbish - she would always give encouragement. I met her in town a couple of years ago and she remembered me from all that time ago.' He also liked music teacher, Mr Paul Johnson, who 'accepted that some pupils wouldn't understand music but he did his best to make sure it was interesting.' Nick was in the school choir which took part in *Noye's Fludde* at St Margaret's Church which is mentioned above. The choir also won praise for a performance at St Andrew's Hall in Norwich and were treated to a trip to Oxburgh Hall. Perhaps the person at school who had the most influence on Nick was Mr Dick King, who was a 'very good teacher' of metalwork and, together with his father, inspired him to become an engineer. One incident involving Mr King concerned a boy who had got a cheap fairground ring stuck on his finger and was causing it to swell. Mr King slid a small piece of metal under the ring and very carefully sawed it off. The boy fainted. Finally from Nick Fisher's very comprehensive comments on the staff I shall mention Mr Rufus Leggett, who is described as 'a wonderful chap who had a quiet air of authority and hardly ever raised his voice.' In the 1930s Rufus had attended King Edward VII School where he captained both the hockey and cricket teams. He was in the RAF during the Second World War and at Gaywood Park sported a handlebar moustache.

Another pupil from this period who remembers Gaywood Park's success in sport, especially basketball, and winning the best school-choir competition in Norwich is Eric Steinacker (1964-69). Writing in the special edition of *The Gaywood Gazette* in 1989, he was complimentary about both Mr Fell and Mr Gent and concluded that it 'was a very good school.'

Some of the sporting and other successes in 1964-65 are mentioned above. However a more systematic account is given below.

Mr Fell was keen to expand the range of sports on offer. As early as November 1963 he told the governors that he hoped to include hockey, rugby, basketball and badminton in the curriculum. By 1966-67 teams competed against other schools in football, rugby, cross country, gymnastics, athletics, volleyball, swimming, cricket and tennis. Hockey was also played using the Girls' School pitches and sticks. Four football teams, two rugby teams and two basketball teams were fielded each week.

In 1964-65 the 1st Xl football team had a reasonably successful season albeit they were beaten in the King's Lynn Shield competition by Alderman Catleugh. The school football captain, Greg Hunter, was signed by Norwich City as an apprentice. The Headmaster was particularly delighted to report that the team had beaten the Grammar School 11-0 at home and 8-0 away. Over the coming years results were mixed. In 1965-66 the U13 team won all their matches and so were awarded the King's Lynn and District Shield. They also beat the Norwich U13 Champions. Unfortunately that year the 1st Xl were not allowed to compete in the higher age group as some of the team were over 15 years old. In the following year the best result was that the U13 were runners up in the local league. However in 1967-68 both the U16 and U15 teams won their local league competitions and three boys, David Serella, Tim Maxwell and John Bushrod, were selected for the county squad. The school field was in a particularly poor condition the following winter and few home matches were played. However two boys were selected for the county squad and David Serella was signed by Nottingham Forest to take up an apprenticeship when he left school. He went on to play for the first team. In 1970, his final year at the school, Mr Fell was pleased to report that the U15 and U13 teams had both won the local shields.

In 1965-66 the school played its first rugby match which was against Glebe House. In only its second season, the following year, the 1st XV won four out of its six matches. A major problem was finding other local teams who played rugby. However in 1967-68 good progress was being made with the senior team winning ten out of thirteen matches and the junior team five out of six. Four boys were selected to play for Norfolk that year and two the following year.

The school regularly entered teams for the King's Lynn and District Cross-Country Competitions. In 1966-67, for example, the juniors came 2nd and 4th out of nine teams and the seniors were 3rd. Two boys were selected to run in the County Championships. The following year the juniors took 1st, 3rd and 7th places and the senior team came 2nd. Three Gaywood Park boys ran in the County Championships.

The school also had a successful gymnastics team and for many years there had been an annual display put on for parents. In 1967 the school provided a team which performed at the Norfolk Show and was filmed by Anglia Television. One group gave a trampolining display which they also performed at a number of local events.

Basketball was for several years the school's most successful sport. In 1966-67 both the U16s, captained by Martin Cork, and the U14s, captained by Timothy Maxwell, won their local leagues

Members of the U14 and U16 basketball teams in 1966-67 (Lynn News)

The 1966-67 U14 Basketball team *(Lynn News). Back row: James Pemberton; Colin Bailey; John Bushrod; Graham Eastwood. Front row: Terence Ramm; Richard Mobbs; Timothy Maxwell; David Serella; Phillip Hewitt.*

and then went on to win the County Championships. Five of the boys were selected to play for Norfolk. In the following two years the U16 team again won the County Championship. In the 1967-68 final they beat Methwold 53-16. Six boys played for the county and Timothy Maxwell was appointed Captain. He was also the first boy from Norfolk to gain a place in the South of England team and had a trial for England.

Eddie Reed - a very talented long jumper

Each year boys were chosen to represent King's Lynn in the Norfolk Sports and some went on to compete at national level, for example Eddie Reed represented the County in the All-England Championships at Hendon in 1964 and was placed 4th in the Long Jump with a leap of 19 feet and half an inch. Similarly in 1967 at Peterborough a Gaywood Park boy came 4th in the Hurdles final. At the County Sports in 1968 Timothy Maxwell gained the Amateur Athletics Association Standard in the Triple Jump and David Serella was successful in reaching the Standard in both the Triple Jump and in the Hurdles.

However the outstanding athlete in this period was Keith Howlett who was one of only eight boys in England to be selected for special coaching following his 2nd place in the 400m final in the All-England Championships at Motspur Park in south-west London in 1969. Keith, together with Gary McClennan, Billy Green and Tony Ford, all from Gaywood Park, also represented Norfolk as the Relay team at the All-England Championships.

In cricket one of the most successful years was 1963-64 when the 1st XI won the County Championship, defeating Acle by ten wickets. A few tennis matches were also played in the summer term from 1966 onwards thanks to the co-operation of Miss Bullock and Miss Dore who allowed the boys to use their courts.

The 1964-65 School Magazine mentioned the setting up of a very popular club for chess and draughts. In addition Mr Fell reported to governors in February 1965 that the following extra-curricular clubs were also flourishing: craft; modelling; photography; guitar playing; physical fitness; and table tennis. At the same meeting the Headmaster said that boxing was now done as a club rather than as a school activity. No explanation was given.

In the summer term of 1966 Mr Fell made an interesting statement to the governors:

'Now that the basic organisation of the school has been completed, good relationships established, public image presented and, I believe, greatly improved, it is now time to turn to the next project. I propose to run internal courses based on outward bound principles.'

He promised that more details would be provided at a later date but the only information which has been found is a reference to a course for Duke of Edinburgh Award candidates at the Fire Station in late 1967 or early 1968.

The Headmaster was also keen to promote cultural activities. At Christmas 1964 the School Choir sung a series of carols at a hospital in Norwich and this was filmed by Anglia Television and shown on Christmas Day. In the following summer term a group was entered in the Norfolk Schools' Music Festival and was awarded a 1st Class Certificate. The Guitar Group was featured on both BBC and Anglia TV. At Christmas 1965 the 5th Year put on a nativity play at an end of term concert which also included carol singing. And in July 1967 the school hosted a very successful Day of Music. The theme of the Festival was *The Sea* and it included participants from all local secondary schools. Choirs, orchestras, bands and soloists all took part.

The boys also had some, albeit limited, opportunities to attend various performances by professional companies, for example in November 1965 the 3rd, 4th and 5th years saw extracts from plays performed by the Theatre Centre Company and in the summer term of 1967 there were visits organised to see both an opera and a ballet in Norwich. An Army Band Concert was attended in the autumn term of 1968 and groups also attended some of the Guildhall 'lunch-time' concerts each year. As well as live performances there were also opportunities to see highly-regarded films. Large numbers of boys were taken to the Guildhall to see *Romeo and Juliet, Animal Farm* and *A Midsummer Night's Dream* in 1969-70.

When Mr Fell arrived at the school in 1963 the number on roll was under 500. It rose steadily each year so that in September 1968 there were 564 boys in the school. By the end of that year the Headmaster told governors that there could be 620 in the school by September. He was not far out as the actual number was 615. This increase in numbers was largely the result of the fact that for some years he had encouraged boys to stay on for a fifth year to take public examinations. Over 50 were due to stay at school in 1969-70, despite the fact that they had to pay for their own examination entries. The total costs for the summer 1969 examinations was £225.

The increasing roll caused major accommodation problems. In February 1969 the Headmaster's frustration with the situation was made very clear to the governors. He told them that the library, the hall, the dining room, the potting shed and his office had to be used for teaching and that more accommodation was essential. He also reminded them that in 1963 he had pointed out that the lavatories in the school were unsanitary and he told them that they still were. The facilities for staff were also unsatisfactory. His annoyance was exacerbated by the conditions of the school field which he said had got steadily worse over the previous six years. Due to flooding it had been out of action for six weeks in the autumn term and already in the spring term for four weeks. He had calculated that some 237 football, rugby and hockey matches had been lost. The governors agreed to press the LEA for major extensions to the buildings, to improve the sanitary facilities and to tackle the drainage problem on the playing field. In July it was reported that new drains had been laid across the field, the LEA had put new accommodation at the Gaywood Park Schools at the top of the priority list for buildings and had agreed to provide two mobile classrooms for the Boys' School for September. Despite the work on the playing field the school Sports Day had to be cancelled for the second year running. In addition the Headmaster felt that he had to advise students that because of the overcrowding they would not be able to stay on to take 'A' levels in 1969-70. Presumably the loss of Mr Gent, who had successfully taught British Constitution, was also a factor in this decision.

The two mobile classrooms were provided for the autumn term 1969 but it was still necessary to use the stage, the dining hall and the potting shed for teaching. The classes were large; most were over 30 and one had 40 boys. The other issue was the shortage of specialist accommodation in science, craft and PE. Extra mobiles were no solution to that problem; the only answer was to reduce the teaching time in those subjects which was not satisfactory. Mr Fell told the governors that he felt that he had always been supported by them and the Divisional Executive but he was scathing about the LEA officers who he felt had not dealt the school a fair hand:

> 'I cannot see that there is any evidence to show that the extra accommodation so vital for maintaining the standards of instruction….is any nearer now than it has ever been….I do not feel that my hardworking staff have been given the accommodation they so richly deserve.'

At the same meeting Mr Fell indicated that he planned to retire as from the end of the spring term 1970. In the event he stayed until the end of the summer term as his successor, Mr T F Shephard, was not able to take up his appointment until September.

At his final Governors' Meeting in July there was a rather bittersweet note. Information had been received that the new buildings he had campaigned for so vigorously and for so long were to become a reality but unfortunately the Headmaster had not been officially informed:

> 'I am indeed greatly pleased to learn (even if it is from the Press that I learned it) that the money needed to provide this school with extra accommodation so grievously necessary has been liberated by the Ministry of Education and Science.'

The governors gave the Headmaster their best wishes for a long and happy retirement but were perhaps a little relieved to see him go. It fell to Miss Bullock to pay a more fulsome tribute to his work at the school. She said that they had worked together over the past seven years in a friendly and co-operative way and she described him as 'a man of great energy and vitality', which he had 'put unstintingly at the service of the boys of Gaywood.' There was also a most complimentary article in the *Eastern Evening News* (14 July 1970):

> 'George Fell, who in seven years has given Gaywood Park Secondary Modern Boys' School a standing in the town it had never aspired to before, retires from teaching today….Mr Fell, who had been a remarkably successful headteacher at Upwell and Downham before he came to Lynn, has given the Gaywood Park boys a respect in themselves through their achievements. He did it in the face of a reputation for toughness that the school has suffered from for years.'

6. Thoughtful leadership by Miss D Bullock, 1952-72

Miss Diana Bullock, B.Sc. (Econ), took up her post in January 1952 and she was Headmistress for the next twenty years. After taking a degree in Economics at Nottingham University she taught in London before coming to Norfolk during WW2 to join the staff of Thetford Girls' Grammar School. Then in 1945 she moved to Lynn to take charge of the Special Experimental Grammar School which was based in the old Technical College on Hospital Walk.

Miss Diana Bullock

During her first few years at Gaywood Park the numbers on roll at the start of the autumn term were over 600 rising to 622 in 1956, but with the opening of the Alderman Catleugh Schools in September 1957 numbers fell back to 559 and then down to a low of 424 in 1963 before rising again to over 500 by 1969.

Life at the school under Miss Bullock in the spring and summer terms of 1952 continued very much as it had under Miss Sherman. There were regular trips into King's Lynn to broaden the experience of the girls: for example to the Guildhall to the 'lunchtime' concerts; to places of local interest such as the docks in February, as part of the 4th year social studies course; and to an exhibition of modern art in July. Visitors went into school to give talks on a variety of subjects, such as one on Hinduism and Islam in February, while in March the Sheriff of Norwich spoke to the 4th year girls about his role and in May he hosted a visit for the girls to see the city treasures. All the usual annual events took place, namely inter-house competitions, inter-school netball and hockey tournaments, the Commonwealth Day celebrations attended by civic visitors, Sports Day, the King's Lynn Schools' Musical Festival, Speech Day, and the Swimming Gala. There was also a residential trip to the Lakes in the Whitsun half term of 1952. Eight girls and seven boys were taken on a walking holiday led by the Headmistress, Miss Eileen Gittens and Mr Robert Stevenson from the Boys' School.

However two events stand out in Miss Bullock's first two terms. The first was a sad one, the death of King George Vl at Sandringham. Along with the Boys' School (and the boys from King Edward Vll Grammar School and girls from the High School) the girls lined the field next to the railway line at noon on 11 February to pay their respects as the train carrying his body to London went past. On a more cheerful note the Headmistress had the pleasure of meeting the Queen Mother and Princess Margaret at the Pageant of St George performed at the Guildhall in July. As mentioned in the section about the Boys' School, the cast formed a guard of honour for the royal party as they walked to the garden after the matinee performance. At the Governors' Meeting in October 1952 Miss Bullock reported that she had been told by Lady Fermoy that 'the Queen Mother had commented with pleasure on the children's courtesy and conduct.'

In future years the pattern of school life would be very much the same as outlined above. However I shall try to identify some of the highlights in sport, drama and music, as well as describing the main school trips and visits.

In the summer term of 1952 there was success in athletics for girls from the school. Two were

Ann Featherby

selected to run in the hurdles for King's Lynn at the Norfolk Sports and then for the county in the All-England Championships in Bradford. Ann Freear came third in her heat in the junior girls' hurdles and Ann Featherby was fourth in the final of the intermediate girls' hurdles. Six girls were selected for the Norfolk Sports in the summer of 1954 and ten in 1955 but in neither year did they progress any further. The following year the Norfolk Sports took place on the Gaywood Park playing fields and some 25 girls from the school took part. Even if girls were not successful every year at county and national level they regularly took top honours in the King's Lynn Sports. In 1958, for example, the Vivienne Ferrier Cup for the outstanding performance in the 13-15 age group was won jointly by Sadie Twite of Gaywood Park Girls' School and Pearl Smith from the Girls' High School. Sadie won the hurdles in a record time of 11.1 seconds and the 11-13 relay team also won in a record 59.4 seconds. In addition, Rosaleen Neal equalled the record time in both the 11-13 100 yards and the hurdles. In 1960 the Vivienne Ferrier Cup went to Arlene Roper who jumped 14 feet 8 inches in the 13-15 high jump competition.

Each year school teams played in netball and hockey tournaments. The most negative comment found refers to a netball tournament in Norwich in March 1952 when the team, according to Miss Bullock, was 'overwhelmed'! In March 1954 the school team came first in the North West Norfolk netball tournament; although they tied with the Covent on points they won by having a higher goal total. One enjoyable spin off for the girls was trips to important matches, for example, to the All-England Netball Tournament in Great Yarmouth at the end of March 1952, and in March 1955 Miss Beryl Coates took a party of 55 girls to an International Hockey match at Wembley. Similar trips took place in later years.

In the late 1950s and early 1960s the school was very successful in hockey. In March 1958 both the 1st and 2nd hockey teams won through to the finals of the Norfolk Secondary Modern Schools' Junior Hockey Shield in Norwich. However, as both teams were from the same school they did not play a final. The following year, despite the fact that the county competition was extended to include grammar schools, Gaywood Park again won the shield, beating Yarmouth High School 4-0. The 1st Xl was also successful in 1960 and 1961, making them the winners four years in a row. In 1959-60 two Gaywood Park girls and one ex-pupil were selected to play for the County. Judy Leeder played left back and Valerie Hudson, then at the Lynn Technical College, played centre half in the 1st Xl and Janet Wilson played for the 2nd Xl in goal. Valerie Hudson, who had been school hockey captain in 1958-59, had also been selected during that year to play for the County 2nd Xl. The team coach, Miss Coates, had herself played hockey for Norfolk. Later in the 1960s the teams were not as strong as they had been as a result of many changes in PE staffing. However in 1971 Miss Bullock told the governors that the hockey and netball teams had a full programme of matches and that it was 'a pleasure to see this aspect of the school work picking up again.'

The 1953 Hockey team

The U15 1st and 2nd Hockey teams 1957-58. *Standing: Doreen Wilkin; Jane Barrett; Diane Watson; Janet Wilson; Doreen Akred; Valerie Hudson; Miss B Coates; Christine Court; Christine Short; Doreen Belcher; Carole Gore; Judy Leeder; Marie Witting. Kneeling: Diane Patterson; Judith Serella; Sandra Unwin; Janet Massingham; Mary Court; Rosaleen Neal; Jennifer Chilvers; Betty Kent; Pamela Warnes; Diane Wells.*

The U15 Hockey team 1958-59. *Back row: Rosaleen Neal; Janet Wilson; Judy Leeder; Christine Short; Judith Serella; Miss B Coates. Front row: Diane Patterson; Jennifer Chilvers; Mary Smith; Valerie Hudson (Captain); Sandra Unwin; Marie Witting.*

In swimming the most successful year was perhaps 1955. At the School Gala Beryl King was the swimming champion and Clarice Howard was the diving champion. A week earlier, at the Norfolk Gala, Clarice was the diving champion in the 13-15 age category and Beryl was selected to swim for Norfolk in the All-England Championships in Ilford. She gained an excellent 3rd place in the 100 yards freestyle race.

One non-sporting contest for which girls were entered was an essay competition in 1960. Form 3A submitted entries under the title, 'What the Commonwealth means to me' and Vivienne Allen won 2nd Prize in the 13-15 age group. She received her prize from the Minister of State for Colonial Affairs, the Earl of Perth. Also in the 1960s and 1970s girls took part in Verse Speaking, Bible Reading and Shakespeare festivals. In 1963 Brenda Williamson won 1st Prize in the U15 category in the Shakespeare competition; Marie Barrett was a finalist in the same competition in 1967. However the most successful year was 1970 when Jean Howling gained a Silver Cup for her bible reading at the Hunstanton Festival and was placed 1st in her age group at the Verse Speaking Festival in Norwich. In addition Jeanette Todd gained an Honours Award in the Shakespeare Festival in Hunstanton. A year later in a Norfolk Safety First poster competition Linda Bates in the 2nd year won both the 1st and 3rd prizes.

The girls' involvement in the St George's Pageant was obviously the highlight of 1952. However in December the French Club performed *Cinderella* for the rest of the school. This was reported without a comment. Perhaps it was too difficult for the majority of girls to understand. In December 1956 when the French Club performed a version of *Sleeping Beauty*, it was just seen by the 'A' forms and 1C. To go back to the autumn term of 1953 there was no drama production, although the 1st and 2nd years were able to see the Boys' School production of *Toad of Toad Hall*. The following summer 24 girls and 24 boys, trained by Miss Coates, performed a country dance in Episode 6 of the week-long King's Lynn Pageant held on the Red Mount Field. In the autumn the whole school was able to watch a film of the Pageant in the Boys' School hall. Surprisingly few references to drama productions in the 1950s and 60s have been found: in December 1955 a production of *Treasure Island* was staged on two evenings; *The Kings of Judea* was put on in December 1960; and in the spring term of 1963 the part-time teacher of speech and drama, Mrs F M Tomlinson, produced two plays, *Michael* and *The Stolen Prince*. It was not until December 1971 that another major production, *The Bride of Seville*, was staged. This was put on by 2nd and 3rd years under the direction of Mrs Calvert. Miss Bullock described it as 'a very gay production.'

Although drama in school seems to have been rather limited, there were opportunities to see productions elsewhere. One has already been mentioned above. In November 1952 the 3rd year girls saw two short plays - *Joan the Maid* and *The End of the Fairy Tale* - at the Guildhall and in the spring of 1954 senior girls went to a production of *Macbeth* and forms 3B and 3C saw a two-act costume drama called *Royal Rescue*. In February 1955 there is a reference in Miss Bullock's Log Book to 'plays at the Guildhall' but with no further details. However from the following autumn groups of girls regularly went to see productions for schools put on by the Caryl Jenner Theatre Company. The normal pattern was for members of 1C and 2C to go to see the plays aimed at primary-school children while the 4A and 4B forms went to the secondary-schools' performances. In October 1957, for example, the younger children saw *The Runaways* and *A Sprig of Rosemary* while the older ones saw *The Room with a Chair* and *Happy Journey*. Another drama group, the Theatre Centre Company, came into school each year from 1965. The plays tended to have a historical theme and were mostly suitable for the girls in the 3rd and 4th years. In 1967 the play was about *The Discoverers*, the following year the title was *The President*, a play about Abraham Lincoln, and in 1968 *The Angel of the Prisons* was about Elizabeth Fry.

Mrs Williams's class in the early 1950s.

Mrs Richardson's class in 1954

Saturday trips by groups of girls and staff to see plays became common after Miss Cynthia Foley (Mrs Youngman), who had been at the school since 1964, was appointed Head of English as from January 1967. The first of many such trips was to see *Much Ado About Nothing* at the Maddermarket Theatre in Norwich in the autumn term of 1968. The following autumn there were visits to the Theatre Royal in Norwich and to Cambridge where they saw *St Joan* by George Bernard Shaw. In the summer term *A Midsummer Night's Dream* was seen at the Maddermarket Theatre. To give just one other example, 4th and 5th year girls were taken to see *Under Milk Wood* by Dylan Thomas in Cambridge in 1971-72.

As well as plays, groups regularly attended the season of celebrity concerts at the Guildhall and in addition there were opportunities to enjoy ballet productions. For many years the Ballet Minerva came to the school and performed, for example in October 1957 the 2nd and 3rd years saw extracts from *Swan Lake* and *Sylphide* and a shortened version of *Hansel and Gretel*. Visits to the school by the company were still taking place over ten years later. Other opportunities to see ballet were also offered, for example in the autumn term of 1962 some 50 girls saw *Hansel and Gretel* at the Guildhall and in April 1963 25 girls went to see *Swan Lake* performed in Norwich. To give just two more examples, in 1971, a party of 2nd years went to the Guildhall to see *Ballet for All* and another group saw the Festival Ballet in Norwich. In the autumn term of 1966 a visiting string quartet, funded by the Education Committee, was very much enjoyed. Miss Bullock said that it was 'of great value musically and educationally.'

Music in the school flourished under Mrs Richardson. In December 1952 the Music Club sang carols at the Guildhall and 1st years entertained the members of the Gaywood Old Folks' Club with carol singing. In March 1954 the School Choir took part in a concert at the Guildhall in aid of the National Children's Home and Orphanage. The Choir were usually entered for the King's Lynn Schools' Music Festival and in 1954, for example, gained a Certificate of Merit for its performance. After auditions during the morning and rehearsals in the afternoon, the Festival concluded with a

The Music Group with Miss Snelling, Mrs Richardson and Mrs Catton in 1959

public concert in the evening. In May 1955 Miss Bullock described the concert as 'very successful' and said that the school hall was 'filled to capacity.' Performances by the Music Club were put on in most years, for example at the end of the spring term in both 1959 and 1960, and in December 1959 there was a concert in aid of the World Refugee Fund which raised £57. The following December the cantata, *The Flower of Jerusalem* was performed as well as the play mentioned

Mrs Richardson and the Music Club in 1971

above, *The Kings of Judea*, by Dorothy Sayers. Among many other performances the school choir sung at the Guildhall at a function in aid of the Children's Society in February 1967 and at the end of spring term they performed the operetta, *The Christmas Rose*. Sharman Pirie (Mrs Kunes) was in the school choir and remembers performances of both *Oklahoma* and *South Pacific*. The photograph of the Music Group in 1971 was provided by Helen Prior (Mrs Rippengill) who is sitting on Mrs Richardson's left.

The first residential trip, to the Lake District, is mentioned above. In the summer term of 1953 there were a number of day outings for various groups, for example, about 100 3rd and 4th year girls and 12 staff went to Derbyshire and there was a 2nd year trip to Castle Acre. From the following year there was a specific outing for each year group: the 4th years went to Cambridge; the 3rd years to Norwich; the 2nd years to Castle Acre; and the 1st years were taken to see contrasting areas around King's Lynn – Marshland, Fenland and Breckland. This pattern was repeated in coming years except that London became the destination for the 4th years in 1955 and the following year the 2nd year trip was to North Norfolk. The Broads were included as well as the North Norfolk coast for the 2nd year outing in 1957. In the 1960s the details of summer outings were not always reported but it seems that they were less comprehensive than in previous years, for example in 1965 the 2nd years were taken to North Norfolk, the 'younger' girls to the Norfolk Show and the 'older' girls to London. In 1969 although the trip for the 2nd years to North Norfolk and also to Grime's Graves, the Neolithic flint mines near Thetford, took place and the 4th years went to London and to the Norfolk Show, the only other trip was one to the King's Lynn Docks for the 1st years. The 5th year in the autumn term of 1970 were taken to London, including a visit to the House of Commons, where they met the local MP, Christopher Fowler. He later came into school to talk to them about his work in parliament. An earlier visit to London in 1961 when the girls met the then local MP, Mr Denys Bullard, is illustrated in the photograph.

The first trip abroad was to Paris in the Easter holidays in 1957 led by Miss Draper, Miss Gittens, Miss Griggs and the School Secretary, Mrs Guyton. Future foreign trips included ones to Austria at Easter 1959 and to Switzerland in 1961. Miss Bullock told governors that 'this kind of experience….is a valuable part of education; it is a pity that not more children can take part in it.' From 1963 the children, along with many from other schools, were encouraged to take part in the educational cruises sponsored by Norfolk Education Committee. In October of that year Miss Griggs took 17 girls on the *Dunera* to Tangiers and Gibraltar. In June 1964 Miss Bullock told the governors that another cruise, this time to Italy and Greece was planned and that the cost for 15 days would be £46.10s. However it is not clear whether or not the school took part. These cruises were thoroughly enjoyable as well as educational. Unfortunately only a small number of children from the school benefited, for example in the spring term of 1968 the Headmistress took a party of only seven girls on a cruise to the Mediterranean.

As well as the summer outings and foreign trips there were also some visits connected with the curriculum, for example in October 1953 two 2nd year classes were taken to Grime's Graves by Miss M Brown. This was a popular trip in future years too and in the 1960 School Magazine 2nd year, Pat Lockley, wrote:

> 'The place I liked best was Grime's Graves, which was a big hole in the ground. To get in it we had to climb down a ladder. It was very dark down there so we each had a torch. Round the sides of the wall there were very small tunnels. We had [on] an old coat or mackintosh because it was chalky in the tunnels. We had to lie on our stomachs and crawl in. The walls were made of flint so we all had some to take home as a souvenir.'

A visit to the Houses of Parliament in July 1961

A group visiting Paris in 1957

Several nature-study trips were led by Mrs Catton: in June 1955 and 1957 she took 1st years to Scolt Head Island on the North Norfolk coast; and in November 1956 she took two 1st year classes to Royden Common; the same classes went on a similar trip the following autumn when they were in the 2nd year.

The tradition of holding Harvest Festival services, Christmas parties for each year group and Easter services, all of which had taken place since the1940s, was continued in the 1950s and 1960s. Gifts from the two services were taken to almshouses and old folks' clubs as in the past. The generosity of the girls and their parents was praiseworthy. At Easter 1954 some 1001 shell eggs and about 70 chocolate ones were distributed; three years later a massive total of 1421 eggs was donated. One innovation was the introduction by Miss Bullock of a Service of Nine Lessons and Carols from December 1952. For two years, in 1954 and 1955, it was held jointly with the Boys' School, the first year at St Margaret's Church and the second at St Nicholas Chapel. In future years however the services were held separately. It would seem that this was because of the big increase in numbers in the two schools in September 1956, up to 700 in the Boys' School and 622 in the Girls' School.

The harvest festival in 1966

Another change made by Miss Bullock was to the school badge. At a staff meeting in November 1952 it was decided that the existing badge would be changed as from September 1954 to include the King's Lynn pelican in turquoise and the letters GPSSG (Gaywood Park Secondary School for Girls.) At another staff meeting in July 1954 it was agreed that that from the start of the autumn term the new 1st years would be allocated to one 'A' form, two parallel 'B' forms and a 'C' form. There would be a senior 'B' form in which the girls were a few months older than those in the junior form but for arithmetic and English the girls would be setted according to ability.

A school magazine continued to be published in Miss Bullock's time, albeit not every year. The printing cost however had become prohibitive and so from 1953 it was normally duplicated in school. A special edition, albeit not called *The Parksonian*, was printed in 1960 covering the year 1959-60 to celebrate the school's coming of age. Miss Bullock's introduction is reproduced below:

'Gaywood Park School now comes of age. In September we shall be twenty-one. In this short life, many changes have been seen, the greatest and most disturbing of which, to the world as well as to the school, was the Second World War which broke out in the very week the school was opened. The even tenor of scholastic days was disturbed by this world shattering war and in many small ways as well as large its presence was felt. Books were not as plentiful, paper deteriorated in quality, school dinners had a more limited menu, evacuees came in, staff were drawn off into wartime occupations, the school gardens became food producing allotments. Nevertheless the school was opened and the girls of King's Lynn had the great advantage of a spacious modern school, set in generous, well-appointed grounds, under the leadership of a resourceful headmistress, Miss K F Sherman, J.P. From 1939-51 Miss Sherman gave the school life and vitality, meeting all the challenges as they came. With the passing of the 1944 Education Act the school passed into the hands of the Norfolk Education

for Housecraft, but was not used for that subject. 'This room might be adapted and equipped as an additional Science room; the other….could with advantage be adapted to serve as a Geography room.'

The inspectors were also critical about the library and the dining facilities:

'The room used as a Library was designed for the purpose and sited away from the busy hub of school life to ensure a quiet atmosphere….However the Library does not play anything like its full part in the life of the school. The main reasons for this are that the room is cold and inadequately furnished, and that there is a serious shortage of books. The room should be equipped so that a complete class can make use of it during library periods….An immediate increase to some 2500 books would meet the minimum requirements for a short period, but when reading and reference work are more generally undertaken that number should be greatly increased.'

Miss Foley's class in 1964-65

The number of books was just over 1000 at the time, well down on the suggested figure.

'The kitchen-dining room is shared by this School and the adjacent Boys' School. It was built to serve from 350-400 meals daily but is now serving upwards of 650….Daily seating accommodation in the dining room is quite inadequate….and meals overflow, in each School, into three or more classrooms….The only solution appears to be the provision of an additional kitchen-dining room so that each School may have its own.'

The comments on the staff however are to a large extent positive:

'The Head Mistress was appointed in 1952, after teaching experience in Selective Central and Grammar Schools. Her general direction of the School, though exercised in an unobtrusive manner, is effective in its results, and in many aspects of the School's work and activities there is evidence of her thoughtful planning and provision.'

'The staff of 23 assistants includes a number of experienced Mistresses (of whom 5 have served in the School since it was opened in 1939) and some young Mistresses of promise. There are several accomplished teachers, but the staff has not yet reached its full potential as a teaching force. There is, naturally, considerable variation both in the approach and methods employed by individual Mistresses and in the effectiveness of their teaching, but the work of the staff as a whole is marked by steady industry and seriousness of purpose….Mention must be made of the valuable work of the Deputy Head Mistress in the general administration of the School and of the close support she gives to the Head Mistress.'

The arrangement of classes into 17 forms and the way they were grouped by ability was said to work well. However it was suggested that a seven-period rather than a six-period day might be beneficial.

Mrs Hammond's class in 1964-65

The section on the school as a community was also complimentary:

'High among her aims the Head Mistress has placed the task of developing a strong corporate life and good social relationships….The friendly and responsive attitude of the girls and the wholesome relationship between staff and pupils are indications of the success which has attended the patient and untiring efforts of the Head Mistress and the staff in this respect. The girls have pleasant manners and, with a few exceptions, take a pride in their appearance.'

'The daily act of corporate worship is conducted in an atmosphere of dignity and sincerity and it is satisfactory to find that the girls are taking a steadily increasing part in the organisation of the service.'

'The House system is developing on good lines….The School Prefects carry out their duties in a praiseworthy manner.'

'There is close co-operation with the Governors and parents and the School enjoys their close support at its well organised functions. Voluntary clubs and societies are not yet well established; this is a valuable aspect of school life which might well now receive increased attention.'

On the curriculum and standards of work there were some critical points made:

'There is no central copy of the syllabus, and the Head Mistress's outline of the schemes does not give sufficient indication of the general lines and content of the courses of work. A revised copy might well include a statement of her aims for the School.'

'The detailed schemes of work have been prepared by the Form or Specialist Mistresses, or by small groups of Mistresses who are closely associated in the teaching of certain subjects. The schemes have, on the whole, been thoughtfully drawn up and the needs of differing abilities have been borne in mind.'

'The School has achieved soundness in fundamental matters and in certain studies, particularly in English and Arithmetic; there is considerable promise about much of the work in several other subjects. The attitude of the majority of girls to their work is good.'

Detailed comments are made on the various subjects and while suggestions for improvement were made the remarks are largely positive. The Report's conclusion is as follows:

'The School has arrived at an interesting stage in its development. It has a vigorous corporate life, good social values and a sense of purpose. There is thoughtful leadership by the Head Mistress and sincere and painstaking teaching by the staff, together with steady effort and a wholesome attitude to work by the girls.'

'Though the work of the School is sound in all essentials certain aspects of it are, as yet, pedestrian and lack the inspiration of a sense of adventure. There are, however, several growing points of considerable promise and a steady advance in quality may confidently be expected.'

In July 1955, at the first Governors' Meeting following the publication, a number of decisions were taken to implement suggestions in the H.M.I. Report:

1. To equip Room 12 as a science room
2. To provide blackout for Room 11 and use it as the geography room
3. To equip the library with tables and chairs so that it could accommodate a class
4. To re-decorate the staff room

However it was sometime before these improvements were realised. 12 tables for the library were not delivered until January 1957 and it was another month before 40 stacking chairs arrived. During the summer holidays in 1957 Room 12 was altered to convert it from a domestic science room to a science room and in December there is a mention of 'further adaptation' being 'made on the new science room in the prefab.' At the end of January 1958 it was reported that work had begun on the new school clinic. An additional canteen, seen as a priority by H.M.I., was finally opened in January 1961 some six years after they had suggested that the need for such a building was urgent. Miss Bullock also adopted the suggestion made by H.M.I. on the number of teaching periods in the day. In the autumn term of 1955 a four-period morning, except on Mondays, was introduced.

At about the same time as these changes were being made, more up-to-date audio-visual facilities were being introduced. In October 1957 Miss Bullock had visited Hellesdon Secondary Modern School to see the television set which was in use there. However it was in the Boys' School that one was installed in January 1958. The schools' programmes were broadcast from 2.05 to 2.30 pm on four afternoons per week and some 80 children, half boys and half girls, watched the 21-

Miss Williams's class in 1966-67

inch set on each occasion. It was said that the reception was good and the broadcasts were well received by the children. One has to wonder how good a view the children got. The Girls' School had got a VHF wireless set in December 1957. Initially rooms 1 to 8, the library and the hall were wired; later one domestic science room and the rooms in the prefab were also connected. However by the spring term of 1961 Miss Bullock had acquired for the school its own 27-inch TV set which was used to watch Geography, French and Current Affairs programmes as well as one for less-able children called *Signpost*.

One criticism in the H.M.I. Report was that clubs and societies were not well established and certainly up to 1955 relatively few mentions of clubs have been found. Two plays put on by the French Club and some activities of the Music Club and the Choir are recorded above. Also an RSPCA Club existed in the early 1950s and in June 1952 it organised a pet show. The 1953 *Parksonian* mentions the French Club, the Music Club, a Geography Club, the RSPCA Club and a Bandaging Club. However in the 1954 and 1955 editions only the Music Club gets a write up. In June 1955, a month after the publication of the H.M.I. Report, it was announced that the following clubs, aimed at 1st and 2nd years, would meet on Thursday afternoons from 3 to 3.45 pm: drama; cane work; embroidery; puppetry; athletics; tennis; flower-arranging; gardening; first aid; French; art; bookbinding; and reading. Some 14 staff including the Headmistress were involved. In November 1956 the science, gardening and flower-arranging clubs went on a visit to a Horticultural Show and the following month the flower-arranging club went to an exhibition by the West Norfolk Flower-arranging Society. It would seem that the H.M.I. comments had been taken on board.

Although behaviour in school was not identified as a problem in the H.M.I. Report, Miss Bullock did express her concerns about it on many occasions to the staff and to the governors. Discussions took place regularly in staff meetings about which girls should not be awarded Leaving Certificates because of poor attendance, attitude or behaviour. There were also times when girls who got in trouble with the police and it was with some relief that she told the governors in December 1954 that 'no girl….has been before the court and no policeman has been in school to deal with any wrong doing since September,' and then in February 1958 that 'it is now years since the policeman or probation officer was in school.' Nevertheless there were continuing problems of poor behaviour. In November 1966 Miss Bullock told staff that she was concerned about the number of girls who were smoking in school and the fact that 'fighting was prevalent.' She said that 'defiance and rudeness' needed to be stopped in the 4th year. Clearly the problems continued as, in February 1967, she told staff she was 'prepared to send out about a dozen letters to parents of girls needing disciplinary action.'

Miss Bullock's concerns about the girls' behaviour led her to call a meeting for the parents of 2nd year girls in the autumn term of 1960 to discuss the problems of adolescence. She told governors that 'the staff and I found it a most rewarding meeting and judging from the comments and letters from parents they did so too.' She said that she planned to make it an annual event. In November 1961 she said she was willing to meet any parents at a mutually convenient time but explained that there were four occasions when they were formally invited into school during a girl's school life: for Speech Day; in the July before they started at the school in the 1st year; at the end of the second year; and at the end of the 4th year. She was sometimes disappointed by the numbers who attended these meetings, for example, at that for prospective parents in July 1963 only 'about one third of the parents availed themselves of this opportunity.' Perhaps surprisingly it was not until July 1967 that the Headmistress announced that she intended to increase the number of parents' evenings so that there was one in each of the years a girl was in school.

Miss Bullock with the Head Girl (Sheila Johnson) and the prefects in 1966-67.

One of the major problems faced by both the Boys' and the Girls' Schools in this period was the difficulty of retaining and recruiting staff. Miss Bullock on many occasions had to change the timetable to cope with staff shortages. In April 1954 she told the governors that 'the lack of surplus women nowadays is having its effect on schools. Our young teachers are marrying quickly, often after the first or second year's teaching.' In the spring of 1958 there were 38 or more children in eight out of the sixteen classes because of the shortage of staff and in the summer Miss Bullock reported that advertisements for vacancies had 'appeared in educational papers fifteen times since the end of August 1957 until the week ending 13 June 1958' and not one applicant had been forthcoming. She said that seven years ago the school had had four PE teachers and that now, with only about 30 fewer children, there was one, Miss Coates. Despite this there had been notable successes in hockey, netball and athletics. This was the second time she had mentioned Miss Coates to governors that year. In the spring she had said that she was doing a valiant job; 'I esteem her work and her standards highly.' On another occasion Miss Bullock told governors that teaching was a much more exacting job than it had been in the past and this was another factor explaining the difficulties of keeping and recruiting staff. She was particularly concerned about the fact that few staff were as good with the less-able children as with bright or average girls. She believed that the 'D' classes should be taught for most of their lessons by their form teacher but when Miss Freeman retired in 1960 she was left with only one mistress able and willing to teach these less-able girls as a class group.

In February 1962 Miss Bullock gave a report to the governors on her first ten years in the school. She said that she felt lucky that she still had on the full-time staff 11 of the teachers who had been in post when she arrived at the school, as well as three on the part-time staff who had previously been full-time. These teachers had given the school stability. One problem was that the curriculum was not covered as well as she would have liked, although she felt that it was reasonable compared with many schools. Bible study, arithmetic, PE and slow-stream children were the least-adequately staffed. In terms of equipment the school was well blessed and the library had 3710 books compared with 'practically nothing' in 1952. She said that over the past decade there had been big changes in girls who grew 'more sophisticated every year.' She felt that they were by and large 'sensible, thoughtful and outspoken' with 'a quick sympathy and generosity.' Good steady work of a satisfactory academic level was done, particularly in the 'A' stream. However as far as the lowest-ability group was concerned, despite all the hours devoted to them by trained teachers, some improve their reading ages in four years by only a few months. Nevertheless in 1966 she told governors that she was pleased with the level of literacy in the 4th year. Only seven girls were still illiterate, that is they had a reading age of less than ten and a half years.

By November 1963 Miss Bullock was pleased to be able to report to governors that the staffing situation was better than at any time since 1952. This had allowed her to introduce a new form of organisation in the first year. The three forms, named after the form mistresses - 1G, 1M, 1R - were completely mixed ability rather than streamed as in the past. For the teaching of English, history, geography, bible study, science and French they were divided into four sets by ability. The girls were put in separate sets for arithmetic. Miss Bullock said that she would like to extend this pattern of organisation to succeeding years if the staffing situation allowed it. She told them that it broke down the barriers between 'A', 'B' and 'C' streams, had some good social effects and was a stimulus to learning. An H.M.I. who had spent three days in the school in October had been particularly interested in this change and approved the principles on which it depended.

The library in July 1970

Another major change came in 1968-69 when Miss Bullock decided not to hold a Speech Day. For many years the governors had paid for a marquee which could accommodate all the girls, parents, staff, governors, civic leaders and head teachers from local schools. However vandalism had become a problem and so, despite her regrets that she would no longer be able to summarise the successes of the school in the previous year to a wide audience, the Headmistress decided to replace the Speech Day in July with an Open Day. This became the norm over the next few years.

Unlike Mr Fell, Miss Bullock had not actively recruited girls to stay on at school for a fifth year. However in 1970-71 there was for the first time a reasonable number who wanted to take CSE examinations and a class of 22 was formed. In the event some 16 took the examinations in the summer and achieved a total of 79 grades, 35% of them at Grade 1, the equivalent of a GCE pass and 58% were at Grades 1 or 2.

Over many years the girls under both Miss Sherman and Miss Bullock had been encouraged to have a social conscience and to help those less fortunate than themselves. The produce from Harvest and Easter festivals had each year been taken to old peoples' homes and almshouses. Many concerts and bring and buy sales had been held for charity. In the summer term of 1970 over 100 girls took part in a 10-mile sponsored walk in aid of the Spastics Society and the excellent sum of £293.66 was raised. It was reported in 1971-72 that girls were doing community service, for example shopping for ladies in Thoresby College and visiting Woodlands Old Peoples' Home. Some had been working in the Oxfam shop on Saturdays in December and each day in the week before Christmas.

During the 1950s and 1960s, as well as frequent changes of staff referred to above, some long-serving teachers left the school. In December 1955 Miss E White left after 14 years' service. Miss Bullock said that she had 'made a sincere and highly individualistic contribution to the work and life of the school.' Miss Kathleen Spinks, who had been at the school since it opened in 1939, retired in December 1957 after 41 years in teaching. The following July saw the retirement of Mrs L M Baker who had also taught at the school since it opened. She had left the Girls' High School

The Girls' School staff in 1967

in 1905 and had taught at St Nicholas's School for thirty years and then at St Margaret's School before moving to Gaywood Park. She told the Lynn News that she had enjoyed her work tremendously and would be very sorry indeed to leave. She said that 'the greatest pleasure I have had is to see the work the girls turned out.' Mrs M A Hitch also retired in 1958 after 13 years at the school. Miss D Freeman who officially retired in 1960 had been on the staff when it opened in 1939. She had left in 1944 but returned in 1953 and she continued to work part-time at the school for some years after her official retirement. One of the other members of the original staff who retired in 1960 was Mrs Gladys Catton who, according to Miss Bullock, had given 'the school unstinted service as a teacher and in many activities too.' In 1964 Miss J Griggs left to teach abroad after ten years at the Girls' School and the following year Miss Ann Dunwoody, who had been at the school since 1948, retired. Miss Bullock described her as an individualist who had worked hard for the school. She said that her influence would remain for a long time, not least in the library which she had built up from a few volumes to 4500. Teri Wright (Randle) says that she was 'a very inspirational teacher' and that she had never forgotten her. Miss Florence Brown, another of the original 1939 staff, retired at Easter 1966.

Miss Bullock was an effective Headmistress. According to Mrs Youngman, she was always calm and never raised her voice but was well respected by the girls. To make sure she knew what was going on in the school she often sat at a desk outside her office or walked around the building looking into classrooms. She was very supportive to staff and girls, for example she usually turned up to see groups off on trips.

In July 1971 Miss Bullock announced that she would retire at the end of the summer term 1972. The decision to merge the two schools under one head teacher had already been taken and she obviously decided that after over twenty years it was an appropriate time to go. The Chairman and members of the Governing Body paid a warm tribute to her 'devoted service to the pupils throughout her appointment and resolved that their appreciation and best wishes for the future be recorded.'

The Girls' School staff in 1971

Even before she retired in July 1972, Diana Bullock had been very involved in the local community. She had joined the King's Lynn Civic Society in 1951 and had served on the executive committee since 1952. For two years from 1977 to 1979 she was Chairman and then for 13 years was the Society's President. When she resigned in 1992 the committee marked her service by commissioning a special bench suitable for use by disabled people. It was originally erected in New Conduit Street with a view of the Customs House but is now in Saturday Market Place. Miss Bullock was also a founder member of the King's Lynn Preservation Trust and helped to set up the Town Guides. She was awarded an OBE in the 1967 New Years' Honours list for services to education and the local community.

Diana Bullock died in 1994 aged 86.

7. From single sex to co-education

There were 78 applications for the headship of the Boys' School to replace Mr Fell and five men were interviewed on 29 January 1970, including the former Deputy Head, Mr R E Gent. Mr Thomas Frederick Shephard, who had been Head of West Walton Secondary School since 1966, was appointed. However, before many months had elapsed, he would find that the job he had applied for and been appointed to would not exist for very long.

Soon after he took up his post Mr Shephard received the news that the Department of Education and Science (DES) had approved a 210-place extension to the two schools at a cost of £125000. When this approval was notified to the governors in November 1970 the Divisional Education Officer drew attention to a number of problems which would arise if the schools stayed single sex. He said that there would be a duplication of accommodation, specialist staff and equipment and that, unless joint accommodation was provided in a central location, a serious circulation problem would result. After much discussion it was agreed that the schools should become co-educational as from 1 September 1972. This meant that the headship of what would be a new school would have to be advertised. In February 1971 it was agreed by the DES that a further 250 places would be provided at an estimated cost of £140522. The proposal to merge the two schools was also approved.

Mr T F Shephard

As it turned out, in July 1971, Miss Bullock announced that she intended to retire at the end of the summer term 1972 and the governors agreed unanimously that Mr Shephard would be the Head of the new school as from September 1972.

During the school year 1971-72 work began on the first phase of the new extension as did minor alterations to the interior of the existing buildings. However two mobiles which had been promised to relieve pressure on accommodation at the Boys' School had still not arrived by November 1971 and some classes were having to be taught in the Girls' School. There was quite a discrepancy in numbers between the two. In September there were 665 boys, up 44 on the previous year, while the number of girls was only 529.

One change that Mr Shephard decided to make soon after he arrived was in the organisation and focus of the examinations. He announced that two-year GCE and CSE courses would be introduced for the 4th and 5th years in September 1971 leading to examinations in the summer of 1973. The RSA examinations would be phased out.

GCE results in 1971 were rather disappointing compared with those in 1970 (shown in brackets):

Number of students:	36 (45)
Number of certificates gained:	74 (99)
Number with 5 or more passes:	5 (10)
Number gaining no passes:	16 (7)

Also in 1970 one boy had achieved an 'A' level pass in Woodwork and 64 pupils had gained a total of 149 RSA certificates.

As in previous years changes in staffing were to be a constant problem. The first major change was at Easter 1971 when the Deputy Head, Mr Trevor Norman left after only two years in post. Mr F T (Larry) Seaman was made Acting Deputy Head and in the new mixed school was to become Second Deputy. The First Deputy Head, appointed as from September 1972, was Mr G N Stringer. Two long-serving teachers were to retire before the re-organisation took place. Mr Donald Macey had been at the school since 1939, except for time in the services during the war. He officially retired in December 1971 but continued to work part time, teaching his geography examination groups until June. Craft teacher, Mr Edgar Haverson, also left at the end of the summer term of 1972.

A major change in the organisation of the new mixed school from September 1972 was the introduction of a year system and appointments were made to head of year and deputy head of year posts before the amalgamation took place. In what was to be a very large school with over 300 in each year group, the Head felt this was the only way to ensure that good pastoral care and academic oversight were provided. It is significant that his reports to the three main governors' meetings each year were written in part by the heads of year. Mr Shephard reported on the buildings, the staffing situation and the organisation and curriculum; each head of year provided reports on matters such as pupil progress, behaviour, trips, music and drama, sporting achievements and fundraising for charity. The Head of PE, Mr Stephen King, also provided a detailed report on sporting activities.

As from January 1973 a new curriculum for pupils in the 4th and 5th years was introduced. All groups would take mathematics, English, RE, PE and practical options. For the more able and average-ability pupils subject options for GCE and CSE courses continued to be available but there were three new courses for average and less-able pupils: Science of Living; Humanities; and Pursuits. The third course included camping, orienteering, climbing, environmental survival and survival swimming, as well as sports such as badminton, table tennis and five-a-side football. It was offered as a two-year course to about half the 4th and 5th years. In 1974-75 two groups were on GSE courses, three on CSE courses, four on the general course, with the possibility of taking a Mode 3 CSE in some subjects, and there were two remedial groups.

In the other years the children were taught in ability bands. In 1973-74, for example, the 312 pupils in the 2nd year were in 11 classes in three bands: B1, B2, B3 and B4; B5, B6 and B7; B8 and B9; and two remedial classes, B10 and B11. As in the past letters were used for each of the year groups so the 1st years were in A classes, the 2nd years in B Classes, the 3rd years in C classes and so on.

From 1973-74, when pupils had to stay on until they were aged 16, special Link Courses based at NORCAT (one day per week) provided further choice for average and less-able children. In that first year 139 out of a year group of 294 were enrolled on courses such as hairdressing, hotel and catering, nursing, engineering and distributive trades. The following year 160 pupils were involved and in addition some 15 spent one day per week on work-experience placements, organised by Mr Huw Price, the Head of the Remedial Department. While this latter number stayed about the same in coming years the number on link courses firstly jumped to 224 in 1975-76 but then fell to around 65 to 70 in the following two years. This would seem to indicate a lack of customer satisfaction with the courses on offer.

A Community Service scheme was also offered to a group of less-able pupils in the 4th year in 1972-73 and this continued when the same group was in the 5th year. The head of year was

Miss Coates and as she rotated as Head of Year 4 or Head of Year 5 over the coming years the scheme continued. The Tuesday Club as it was known in that first year was based in Miss Blatherwick's home economics room and involved old people being entertained to refreshments served by a group of boys and girls. Other opportunities to get involved over the years included help at Fairstead Play Group and Alderman Jackson Special School, digging gardens, chopping wood and helping with Meals on Wheels. However it was the Tuesday, Thursday or Monday Club – its name varied depending on the timetable in a particular year – which was the most important. The numbers of old people entertained each week grew from 16 in 1972-73 to 60 in 1978-79. In that last year £102 was raised in donations from the year group to fund the club's activities which included 'a really first-class Christmas party.' There was a turkey-salad tea at 4.30 pm followed by music-hall entertainment provided by the Black Velvet Concert Party. Presents and cake were also provided. On more than one occasion Miss Coates expressed the hope that another year group would take on the Old Folks' Club but none took up the idea and so with the invaluable help of Miss Eileen Blatherwick she had continued to run it.

The Old Folks' Club was one of the means by which the school reached out to the local community. When Mr Shephard first took on the headship he found that the parents were very reluctant to come to meetings and were not very supportive of what the school was trying to achieve. However things improved considerably over the years. One major improvement came with the appointment of an education welfare officer who was well known and respected by local people. In a number of ways the Head worked to encourage pupils to be more committed to their school, for example he involved them in staff appointments. Each interviewee was sent around the school with some pupils who were later asked for comments on the candidates they had accompanied. One stratagem aimed at stopping school notices being defaced was to exhibit large numbers of pieces of pupils' art work around the school labelled with their names. This seemed to have a very positive effect. On one occasion when he was covering a lesson for a craft teacher Mr Shephard noticed that a chisel was missing when they were clearing up since every tool had its place. To force the culprit to own up all the pupils were kept back so that they missed their break and were also made to stay in after school. Still the chisel did not appear. When the teacher came back next day and confessed he had taken the chisel home, Mr Shephard was mortified and made a point of apologising individually to each of the boys in the class.

Considerable disruption in the running of the school over a number of years was caused by the major work to remodel existing buildings and to provide additional accommodation. The start of the autumn term in 1972 was delayed for a week as the toilets for the new co-educational school had not been completed. However this had a very positive effect in that it allowed time for meetings of subject departments and year teams and helped staff from the Girls' School and the Boys' School to get to know each other. In that first term both dining areas had to be used for teaching but by January 1973 the first part of the new extension was ready and the second part was in use in the autumn term. Ten additional teaching spaces, a new library and a study room had been provided. By the spring term a new area for art with four teaching spaces was in use and a start had been made on a third building phase, the provision of a sports hall and changing rooms. The raising of the school-leaving age (ROSLA) to 16 in 1973-74 meant that even more accommodation had to be planned. During 1974-75 good progress was made on the building of the sports hall and the new home economics suite and work was also taking place on the conversion of classrooms in the south wing into a biology laboratory. In the autumn term of 1975 the new sports hall came into use as did three of the new HE rooms. The old domestic science rooms in the north building were being renovated to provide additional science rooms and when this work was completed at the beginning of June 1976 the level of accommodation for the subject was considered to be good. Despite all these new buildings the school was to need even more accommodation in the next few years. Two mobiles were allocated to the school in the autumn term of 1976 to compensate for rooms used by the Western Area Tutorial Unit and a further three mobiles were provided the following October. These were used for the teaching of French and German.

When Mr Shephard took on the headship of the new combined school he faced a major logistical challenge. The numbers on roll in September grew from 1269 in 1972, to 1540 in 1973, to 1600 in 1974 and to 1681 in 1975. By the autumn term of 1978 there were 1748 pupils and it was the largest secondary modern school in the country. The increasing size of the school meant that staffing issues were perhaps even more of a problem than at any time in the past. When the school opened in September 1972 it was fully staffed but in terms of specialist teachers it was out of balance, having a shortage of both mathematics and science teachers. One shock was the sudden death of music teacher, Mrs Blanche Richardson shortly after being taken ill on the first day of the new term. Another long-serving member of the Girls' School staff, Miss Eileen Gittens, had been absent since the previous April following a road accident. Over the next few years she had a number of absences because of continuing back problems, for example in March 1976 she returned to work after being off for 19 weeks with back strain and sciatica.

Some very experienced staff were to retire over the next few years. The first to go was Miss Gwen Williams in July 1974 after 35 years at the school and Deputy Head since 1944. The staff and pupils presented her with a silver tea set, a coffee set and a trolley. She was replaced by Mrs P Linley as from January 1975. In July 1976 Mrs Queenie Williams and Mr Jock Guy retired. Both of them had been on the staff when the schools opened in 1939, although Mrs Williams had left for a few years when her son was born and Mr Guy had served in the forces during WW2. They had held senior posts in the combined school: Mrs Williams had been one of the five Heads of Year; and Mr Guy had been Head of the Science Department. At a reception they were presented with cheques on behalf of staff, former students and former colleagues and Mr Shephard thanked them warmly for their many years of service. Miss Sherman and Miss Bullock were both present at the reception as a mark of their respect for Mrs Williams and to thank her for her dedication and

Mrs Williams and Mr Guy

commitment.

However the main problems were caused by actual staff shortages, particularly in 1973-74 and 1974-75. At the start of the autumn term of 1973 the school was four staff short and another teacher was due to leave at Christmas. In addition the new staff included 13 probationary teachers straight from college. At one point during the year the school was nine teachers short and children were having to be sent home. Some 30 classes or 900 children were affected. At the end of the summer term 13 permanent staff and three temporary teachers left for a variety of reasons. Although the school was entitled to have 72 teachers, by 10 June only 52 had been retained or recruited for 1974-75.

The disruption continued in the autumn term of 1974 with some children starting late and others being sent home early. The Head reported to the governors in November that 85 teaching units were being lost each week. The problem of shortage of teachers was made worse by increased absenteeism as a result of the extra burden carried by the staff. In the spring term the school was short of nearly ten teachers and in May the problem got into the national press and was even on the ITV news. One headline referred to Gaywood Park as 'the worst school in Norfolk.' As a result of the bad publicity the LEA agreed that the school should be recognised as one in special circumstances. This meant that a number of posts of responsibility were upgraded and the school was allowed to employ four additional teachers. As a short-term measure staff from NORCAT were drafted in to cover some classes, although how successful they were is questionable. In May 1975 the governors were forced to issue a statement regretting the biased reporting in the press and on television, pointing out that the staffing situation was improving and that the school was 'now near the level of full-time education for all children.' They acknowledged 'the difficulties experienced by the staff and the pupils over a difficult and prolonged period of building operations.' However they stated that they had 'every confidence in the future of the school.' How the information had got into the press is unclear but the governors wrote to one of the teacher unions complaining of a release of confidential information to the media. They also complained to the Independent Broadcasting Authority that a film had been taken on the school premises without permission.

On the positive side a number of parents wrote to the local press defending the school. Excerpts from two examples are cited below:

'May I through your columns protest at the adverse criticism thrown at Gaywood Park School? That such reporting, without first checking facts, should take place surprises me. The criticism was and is so broad as to be laughably shallow. No parent will deny that problems exist in schools today. Gaywood is certainly no worse than any school of a comparable size....the problems such as they are have been blown up for the sake of sensationalism.....As a parent I am delighted with the progress of my child.'

'If any child is keen enough to learn, Gaywood has almost every facility there to encourage them.... we do not deserve the publicity Gaywood Park has received. The teachers there do a marvellous job.'

In addition some 120 senior pupils signed a statement which concluded by saying that the school was 'a happy, friendly and caring place and we can honestly say that we have enjoyed the past five years at this school and would never want it changed.'

Although some teachers did not stay long at the school because they found some children difficult to teach, many spent much of their teaching careers at Gaywood Park and found the work very rewarding. Others left for promotion or to have children. Christine Clarke, who taught geography from 1974 to 1980 says that she has many very fond memories of the time spent teaching at Gaywood Park, both of the pupils and of the staff:

'Teaching could be challenging, but also very rewarding, and pupils were both respectful and cooperative, especially over time as knowledge of their difficulties and needs grew with the ability to give them the support they required. I still have happy memories of many of them now, especially when it came to teaching their grandchildren in later years. I would not have wanted to have missed any of my time there.

From the very start there was a welcoming staff, a cross section of younger and more experienced colleagues. I always felt that the challenge of the school focused staff as a close-knit team working for and supporting one another, trying to achieve positive outcomes for all pupils....Many may not have a good word for the old Gaywood Park, but I'm not one of them. Special days.'

In the 1989 edition of *The Gaywood Gazette*, mentioned in previous chapters, Angie Hastings (1973-80) apologised for listening to rumours before she started at Gaywood about it being a rough school. She asserted that it was not and that she was 'proud to tell people where she went to school.' She said that she 'came away from Gaywood with an appreciation of good music....and a great love of literature.' She particularly enjoyed English with Rufus Leggett and Bob Layton and was endlessly grateful to the latter for the trips he organised to Stratford, London and the Lake District. She said a special 'thank you' to Mr Roger Lines 'for the Gershwin.'

Another major staffing problem occurred at the end of the spring term of 1978 when there was industrial action by teacher unions across the country. Over a period of eight days some 72 teachers at Gaywood Park withdrew from voluntary lunchtime duties and after-school meetings. It was a very difficult time for school leaders.

Inevitably the school experienced discipline problems with some pupils. The Head told governors in February 1974 that, so far that year, 19 pupils had had to be withdrawn from one or more classes because of 'perpetual disruption of the lessons concerned.' When withdrawn they were taught by senior staff. Also a supervised work session was operating each evening for those not working satisfactorily in normal lessons. Heads of year sometimes commented in their reports to governors on the poor behaviour of a minority of pupils. In 1978, for example, Mr W Ferguson reported that the 5th year carol service 'was marred by the immature behaviour of a small anti-social minority.' As well as detentions, short-term and occasionally permanent exclusions and corporal punishment were the main sanctions used.

Not only could pupils be a problem; parents too could be very aggressive if they felt their child was being unfairly treated. They would go into the school and cause a disturbance such that the police sometimes had to be called. On one occasion a man was prosecuted for pushing the Head who was trying to prevent him from finding a head of year who had punished his son. The result was that the parent was fined and banned from setting foot in the school unless specifically invited to do so. On another occasion a very explosive situation involving the Head and a parent, who had clearly been drinking, was defused by Mr Larry Seaman. They were well known to each other and Mr Seaman reminded the parent of an occasion when, as a member of a gymnastic display team, he had caught his foot in a vaulting horse and fallen flat on his face. Larry told the man that he was making a greater fool of himself on this occasion than he had then. The result was that the parent, somewhat chastened, left before the police arrived to deal with him.

A huge effort was made to raise the profile of the school in the eyes of the local community, for example in March 1977 the *Lynn News* published a lengthy article entitled:

Gaywood Park shows off its new image:

'Once branded with a name for violence, vandalism and academic failure, Lynn's Gaywood Park Secondary School is giving its critics a chance to come and see for themselves that it now has a completely new image. Headmaster Tom Shephard has so much confidence in the school's 'new style' that he has arranged a display of his pupils' work at the Lynn's King Street Museum as proof of the change.

This new found confidence does not only lie with the staff, the pupils are right behind their Head and agree that problems of previous years no longer exist. Fifth formers, Michael Stone and Keith McKenzie have noticed several changes since first-year days: 'When we first came you could not walk down the corridors without getting pushed about or hit by the fifth year and you had to get out of their way or you were for it' said Michael…. 'Things seem a lot stricter now. The teachers are making sure we are more disciplined' said Keith.'

The article describes the wide range of courses on offer, the fact that the school is fully staffed and the dedication of the teachers.

However in the late 1970s the school still suffered from a considerable amount of theft and/or vandalism in the evenings and at weekends. In 1977-78, for example, there were 12 occasions when the school was broken into or windows smashed. The cost of replacing glass alone was £1342.63. During the Easter holidays there were major thefts of audio-visual equipment on two successive nights. Some £1500 worth of equipment was stolen.

Mr Shephard tells an amusing story about his attempts to reduce theft and vandalism. He decided to have a security system installed in the school since a company had offered to provide it free in the hope of generating interest from other schools. While awaiting the installation of the new system the police agreed to place two alarms in the school linked to the police station. The Head did not tell anyone about this arrangement, as a consequence of which the Deputy Head, Geoff Stringer, in school on a Sunday afternoon to record a video for use in a lesson the following week, was startled by the sudden appearance of four policemen. However the police attendance was not in vain; while they were there they heard a noise on the flat roof and managed to catch two primary-aged boys who were attempting to break in.

During the period of Mr Shephard's headship no external inspection of the school took place and detailed examination results for each year have not been found. It is therefore difficult to say how successful the school was academically. In 1975 there were 85 GCE 'O' level passes and 22 results which were unclassified. Of the 555 CSE grades achieved, 79 (14.2%) were at Grade 1, the equivalent of a GCE pass, and 76 were unclassified. For 1976 no comparable figures are available although some individual subject grades have been found. There were, for example, 53 entries in English at 'O' level and the pass rate was 35.8%. In mathematics 56.2% of the 23 who were entered passed. 7.6% of the CSE passes were at grade 1. The only information found on individual pupils' examination results comes from the summer 1979. Adam Wojcik achieved 4 Grade As and 6 Grade Bs at 'O' level, as well as a Grade 1 CSE pass, a very good set of results. We also know that 18 pupils from that year group stayed on to take 'A' levels in the school's first sixth form.

Adam Wojcik transferred to NORCAT to take his 'A' levels and later studied Metallurgy and Material Science at Imperial College in London. He completed a Ph.D. in 1989 and then worked in the scientific instrument industry for six years and as a visiting lecturer at Imperial College before being appointed a Lecturer at University College London in 1995. Although he did not stay on at school to do his 'A' levels he nevertheless recognises a debt that he owes to the staff at Gaywood Park:

'I really owe a debt to that school and, in particular, my teachers, who encouraged those that were receptive, to get on….They were all great, and I have fond memories of them all – from Metalwork to Maths, Technical Drawing to Art, Needlework to Domestic Science, and from British Constitution to British Social and Economic History. I still have my copper ashtray, painstakingly made over many weeks in metalwork - in that gloomy hut off the southern playground - a testament to what was still regarded as politically correct and socially acceptable at the time!

My parents were mortified that I had to go to GP, as this was the notorious "rough" school in King's Lynn. I came from the top set in St James' primary school, and the entire class failed their 11 plus in what was a seismic event for a school – all as a result of a disastrous teacher, who spent his time talking about politics. I think he left teaching and later became a labour party candidate. The parents were up in arms, and a deputation took a coach to the LEA in Norwich to campaign to get us into the grammar school, but it was not to be.

In hindsight, however, failing the 11 plus and going to GP was probably the best thing that could have happened to me. I reckon I would have been a very small fish in a big pond had I gone. However, in saying this, I recognise that I could well have performed below my potential at GP, had it not been for the teachers there. That was the key, in my eyes at least, that was able to drag success from the jaws of a perceived (but perhaps overdone) educational disaster. I carry this thought with me to this day - it has influenced my own teaching for the past 30 years that I have been a lecturer at university level (which I acknowledge is less of a battleground). I believe that teachers hold an immense power in their hands, which if appropriately used, can make a massive difference to one's life chances. I don't think they even realise how significant they can be.

At GP, I don't recall much roughness, but there were pupils who were clearly unteachable. I was never targeted (well, not seriously) for bullying, despite being your "classic" bookish/nerdy teenager. I recall sitting in on an English class when our normal teacher, Robert Layton, was absent. The poor fellow in charge was unable to hold it together, and one of the more notorious pupils actually faced up to him, in a very ugly way. We all knew the score in parts of the school. I think when I joined, the slipper was still being used, but then went out of fashion, certainly whilst I was there, and this had an effect on discipline. Robert Layton dealt with this in an amazing way, and could reduce even the worst offenders to a quivering mess, simply by the power of his sarcasm and wit. Others had different ways. Our physics/chemistry teacher simply inspired us all with his dancing atoms, and his super thick spectacles. It is to them, that I owe a great deal of gratitude.'

Under the leadership of the Head of PE, Mr Stephen King, the school was highly successful in a range of sports in the 1970s. Teams were fielded in football, rugby, basketball, hockey, netball, cross county, athletics and cricket and many trophies were won at district and county levels. There were some very talented individuals who were selected to play for Norfolk and in some cases for regional and national teams. Complete information on sport at the school up to 1979 is not available but the following paragraphs describe many of the major highlights.

The school was able to field five football teams each week with the help of non-PE staff such as Mr Barry Chandler and friends of the school like Joe Feeney, the owner of the newsagents in Gaywood. 1973-74 was a particularly successful year. The U15s won the West Norfolk (Britannia) Shield for the fourth time in five seasons but more importantly won the Tom Easthall Cup for the first time when they beat Alderman Leach School in Gorleston 4-1 in the county final at Carrow Road. David Goose and Robert Linford were selected to play in the County U15 side and both

The 1970-71 Britannia Shield Winners *(Lynn News). Back row: Richard Johnson; Glen Brundle; John Hyam; Mr B Chandler; Paul Burch; Trevor Rye; Alistair Reeve. Front row: Steve Alford; Michael Jones; Ian Cawston; David Muncaster (Captain); John Overton; Stephen Everitt; ? Woods.*

joined Norwich City on schoolboy terms. The following year was perhaps even more successful. All the teams won the area championships and the U15s retained the Tom Easthall Cup, beating Blyth Jex 4-1 in the final of the county competition. The U16s won the county section of the English Schools' Individual Championships and represented Norfolk against Henry Fanshawe School in Derbyshire, unfortunately losing 2-1. Robert Linford and David Goose were again selected to play for the county, this time at U19 level. They also had the honour of being two of eight boys from Norfolk chosen to act as ball boys at an England v Portugal match at Wembley on 20 November 1974. In contrast the 1975-76 season was not a great one. However Peter Mendham and Robert Carter played for the Norfolk Schools' U19 side and both were offered apprenticeships by Norwich City FC. Peter became a Norwich 1st team player. He returned to the school in December 1978 to present the Tom Easthall Cup, won the previous season, to the U15 football captain, Gary Davenport, who had been in the winning team which beat Oriel School in Great Yarmouth by 7 goals to 2.

Another outstanding sportsman was Jody Huizar who made the County U15 rugby team when he was in the 3rd year and the following year (1972-73) won a full England cap having been selected to play loose-head prop for the U15 team. In September 1973 the President of the Norfolk Rugby Association visited the school to present Jody with a cup 'for the person who has done most to further the advancement of rugby football in the county' in the previous season. This was the first time the award had gone to a schoolboy. Perhaps it is not surprising that in 1973-74 the school U15s won 10 out of their 11 matches. That year several boys were selected to play rugby for the

The 1977-78 Tom Easthall Cup Winners (Lynn News). *Back row: Alan High; Clive Woods; Mike Smith; Chris Fox; Nicholas Tatnell; Ian Ferguson; Kevin Hardy. Front row: Steven Perry; Kevin Schmuda; Richard Ward; Michael Docherty (Captain); Gary Davenport; Stephen Brassett.*

Peter Mendham and Gary Davenport

Jody Huizar and his England Schoolboys' Rugby Cap in 1973 with Mr Stephen King

county: Jody Huizar for the U19 XV; and David Hooks, P Neale and Ian Weir for the U15s. In addition Jody and Ian played for the Eastern Counties and Jody was again capped for England, playing in the U16 XV. In April 1974 he toured France with the England squad. The following year the school team were the first winners of the Frank Judd Shield, beating Stanground Secondary School in Peterborough 11-7 in the final of the competition. Although rugby continued to be played, a rather telling comment was made in a report to the governors in July 1977: the sport has ticked along but has had 'little success or real drive since Huizar's time.'

An all-round sportsman, Jody Huizar also played for the U16 SE England basketball team and was a very competent hammer thrower. In the Six Counties athletics match at Luton in July 1974 he beat all opposition and his own previous best performance by throwing an excellent 53.12m in the Intermediate Boys' event. A week later in the All-England Championships in Shrewsbury he came a very creditable fourth.

Jody Huizar and some of the rugby team in 1973

Basketball was another sport in which the school was particularly successful. In 1972-73 the boys U16 team won the County Championship, beating Wymondham in the final. Five boys were selected to play for the County U15s and four for the U14s. The girls' U16 team won the area league despite having only played for six months. The following year the U16 boys again won the County Championship, this time beating Greenacre School in Gorleston. As mentioned above Jody Huizar was selected to play for SE England. In addition Raymond Fox and David Goose played for the County U15s and Robert Carter and Paul Berney for the County U14s. The girls' U16 team were county finalists and both Karen Nazar and Sandra Holland played for Norfolk. The boys' teams were very ably coached by Mr Tony Gayton and the Girls' teams by Miss Jenny Clarke.

In 1974-75 the girls' basketball teams - the Demons (U16s) and the Dwarfs (U14s) - won both the county trophies for the first time. Five girls were selected to play for the county at U16 level. In addition there were four boys in the county U15 and three in the U14 squads. Although I have not found a definitive statement to the effect, it would seem that both boys' teams won in their respective county finals in 1974-75 as the information for the following year refers to them defending their titles for the third successive season. In the event the U16s lost in the semi-finals to the eventual winners and the U14s reached the final but had to concede the game 'due to unfortunate circumstances.' The mind boggles! The 1975-76 season was again a successful one for the girls' teams. The Demons won the County Championship and the Dwarfs were beaten finalists. In the English Schools' Basketball Association individual schools' competition, the U16s reached the semi-finals but lost to Firth Park School in Sheffield while the U14s got to the final but lost over two legs to Dayncourt School in Nottingham. Five girls – Jackie Brennock, Kay Brennock, Gillian Pope, Colleen Smith and Vivienne Whiley - were selected to play for the county and one of them, Jackie Brennock, played in the South East of England U16 team, although she was not 14 until March. The basketball teams also had success in 1976-77. In the autumn term, as well as Jackie

The 1977-78 U16 Girls' County Basketball Champions (Lynn News). *Back row: Lorraine Degnan; Teresa Parrish; Jane Waterfield; Linda Schmuda; Teresa Sturman. Front row: Lynette Sherring; Kim Card; Angela O'Toole (Captain); Jackie Brennock; K Curtis; Miss J Clarke.*

The 1977-78 U14 Boys' County Basketball Champions *(Lynn News). Back row: Nigel Smith; Clive Jarvis; Carlis Benjamin; Martin Lindsay. Front row: Richard Brown; Russell Howling; Clive Bush; Karl Hinzer; Chistopher Taylor.*

Brennock, two other girls, Angela O'Toole and Lorraine Degnan, played for the South East of England. Both girls' teams won the county titles, as did the boys' U16 team – the Gladiators. The following year the U16 girls had a convincing win over Wymondham Secondary School beating them by 59 points to 20 to take the title yet again, the boys' U14 team narrowly beat Thorpe St Andrew 37-36 to take the *Lynn News and Advertiser Shield* but the U16 boys lost to Norwich Royals 42 to 51.

Jackie Brennock (1973-78) was one of Gaywood Park's outstanding sportspersons. In January 1977, as a 14-year old, she played in the England U15 Basketball Team which thrashed Scotland 51-25 on their own ground. Two months later she helped England to a 62-32 defeat of Wales. After these two appearances she was named England Vice-captain. She was the *Lynn News and*

Jackie Brennock, the 1977 Sportswoman of the Year (Lynn News)

104

Advertiser Sportswoman of the year in 1977. In September 1978 Jackie, by then at NORCAT, was awarded a Certificate of Merit by the Physical Education Association for outstanding service to PE. Not only had she played for England at basketball, she had qualified as a referee and had helped to train Gaywood Park teams.

In cross-country running too, members of the school got to take part in county and national competitions. In 1972-73 the outstanding performers were 1st year, Vivienne Whiley, and 2nd year, Hazel Benjamin, both of whom represented Norfolk in the All-England Championships. The following year both the boys' and the girls' teams did well in the King's Lynn and District and County runs and Linda Seapey, Tony Hunt and John Mendham were selected to represent Norfolk in the national championships. Peter Mendham, mentioned above was an all-round sportsman and as well as football he represented the school in athletics, basketball and cross country. He also ran for Norfolk in the All-England Cross-country Championships at both Derby in 1975 and Portsmouth in 1976. In 1977 four boys, one of whom was Stephen Watson in the 4th year, were chosen to represent the county. Unfortunately the names of the other pupils have not been found.

Similarly information on athletics is scant. In the summer of 1974 Gaywood Park pupils made up more than half the King's Lynn boys' team and over one third of the girls' team which competed in the County Championships. Three pupils were chosen to represent the county at the All-England Championships, one of whom was Jody Huizar as mentioned above. In 1975-76 there was said to be a high level of interest in athletics. In the County Championships, Sean Bristow (in the 1500m) and Ray Venemore (in the 100m and long jump) were 'outstandingly successful' and were selected to take part in the All-England Championships at Cannock.

Another of the school's star sportsmen was Robert Carter. As early as 1973 when he was in the 2nd year he was selected to play for the Norfolk U15 cricket team which Mr King said in his report to governors was 'an excellent achievement for so young a boy.' The following year the school's U15 cricket team led by Robert won the Calder Cup when they put out Watton, the previous holders. Robert was selected to play for the Norfolk Schoolboys' team and was the leading run scorer as well as performing well as a bowler. In the summer of 1975 he captained the Norfolk U15 team which won five out of its eight matches and was also selected to play for both the Midlands Counties Xl and the England U15 team. As mentioned above, in his 5th year Robert played county football and was offered an apprenticeship at Norwich FC. However he gave up football for his first love, cricket, and a newspaper report in January 1979 refers to him playing in the England U19 Cricket Xl in Australia and having been signed by Northants to play county cricket. Not only did he play for Northants but he later became one of their coaches. After working in Holland and Scotland, as well as with Northants, Bob Carter became part of the New Zealand coaching team in 2012.

Hockey and netball matches were also played but in general were less popular and less successful than the sports already described above. However it would be remiss of me to fail to mention Linda Bunn who was selected to play hockey for Norfolk in 1972-73 and Colleen Smith and Paula Etherington who played netball for the county in 1974-75.

The other major sporting successes over a number of years in the 1970s were in weightlifting. The boys were coached by Mr H W Price, the Head of the Remedial Department from September 1973. In 1973-74 twelve boys competed for the first time in the Eastern Counties Championships and five boys were selected to lift for the East Midlands in a match against the West Midlands. Two of them, Richard Switek and Tony Eagle were included in the British Schoolboys' team. The following year five boys qualified for the British Schoolboy Championships in Hounslow. Richard came first in the flyweight class and Keith McCowan in the 44kg class, as a result of which both were selected to take part in an international match at Mannheim in Germany on 26 July between Britain, France and Germany. Out of some 120 competitors, the Gaywood Park boys came 9th and 34th, very creditable performances as they were among the youngest taking part. In March, following his success in Hounslow, Richard Switek appeared on BBC Look East, Anglia TV and Blue Peter.

1975-76 was an even more successful year for Richard. Together with Keith McCowan and Jamie Preston he competed for the East Midlands in the All-England Championships and gained the flyweight title. McCowan was 2nd in the flyweight class and Preston was 2nd in the bantamweight class. Richard retained his title in the British Schoolboy Championships. He was chosen as the *Lynn News and Advertiser* Sportsman of the Year and appeared on the ITV programme, *Magpie*. He was also awarded a trophy as the East Midlands 'most promising lifter.' Later in the year Richard was a member of the English Schoolboys team and in a match against Wales he beat his opponent by 44 lbs. In the British Junior Championships (for U20s) he came 2nd in the bantamweight class, breaking two British records. Following this performance, he and Mr Price were interviewed for six and a half minutes on BBC Look East. In another international match in the summer Richard came 4th out of over 100 competitors.

I shall now describe some of the non-sporting opportunities offered to pupils. Music and drama productions in the 1970s were often organised by the different year groups. In April 1973, for example, there was an informal evening for parents of children in the 3rd year at which some 200 visitors were entertained to excerpts from the World War 2 drama, *The Long, the Short and the Tall* by Willis Hall, songs by the year choir accompanied by guitars and recorders, as well as to a PE and gym display. The following year a mummers' play was organised by Miss Hill for the 1st and 2nd years, while in December 1975 the 3rd year drama club performed *Christmas through the Window*, a modern interpretation of the Nativity. There were also some major school productions,

See How They Run in March 1976

Rope in March 1977 (and right)

some of them directed by Mr Bob Layton, the Head of English: *See How They Run* by Philip King in March 1976; A Christmas Carol in December 1976; and Rookery Nook by Ben Travers in January 1979. In addition, *Rope* by Patrick Hamilton in March 1977 was directed by Mr Bob Rogers and *She Stoops to Conquer* by Oliver Goldsmith in December 1977 was directed by Mr Trevor Knights.

There was also a major musical production at the end of the summer term of 1976. Some 150 pupils were involved in the first musical extravaganza since the amalgamation of the Boys' and Girls' Schools. The concert was in two parts. In the first there were performances by string, brass, recorder and folk groups as well as the senior choir. This was followed by a production of *Captain Noah and his Floating Zoo* which combined the talents of both the music and art departments led by Head of Music, Mr Roger Lines, ably assisted by art teacher, Mrs Joan Skipper. All the scenes

A Christmas Carol in December 1976

She Stoops to Conquer in December 1977

were painted by the children and then turned into slides which were projected onto a screen behind the performers. Some 250 children, parents and friends enjoyed the evening.

Year choirs and a senior choir including members of staff performed at the annual carol services which were either organised for a particular year group or as joint celebrations by two year groups. In December 1978, for example, there was a Festival of Carols including 1st and 2nd year pupils and attended by about 160 parents.

Some extra-curricular clubs were also mainly for particular year groups, although ones organised by the music and PE departments such as the guitar club, the recorder group, the brass band and the gymnastics club went across all year groups and were very well attended. The band which in 1976 was referred to an 'embryo brass band', was so popular that a year later there were more people wanting to join than there were instruments available. After-school clubs specifically for first-year pupils were particularly popular. In 1976 a chess club was formed by Mr John Belfield and Mr Michael Lancefield. The latter was also instrumental in setting up a book club which allowed children to buy books at discounted prices. By the summer term of 1977 there were 90 pupils supporting two book clubs. In addition a woodwork club was run by Mr John Jones and Mr Chris Bowers on one night per week and there was a year choir, trained by Mr Roger Lines and Mrs Watson. These clubs for first-years continued the following year and the choir was over 40 strong in the autumn term of 1977.

In the late 1970s an important activity for senior pupils was the Young Enterprise Scheme. Local businessmen such as Michael Ison, a director of Dynatron in King's Lynn, were involved in helping pupils set up small businesses. Groups then took part in local and regional competitions. In May 1979 the Gaywood Park School company, 'Achievers' Crafts', appeared on the children's television programme *Magpie on ITV*. They took samples of the products they had made, which included mug trees and spice racks, to London.

School magazines had been regularly produced in the Girls' School but only one example, for the school year, 1964-1965, was published in the Boys' School. In the autumn term of 1975 a new magazine, *The Gaywood Gazette* came into existence. It was edited by English teacher, Mr John Wooll and its aim was to give the pupils a chance to have their say about the school as well as to contribute articles, jokes and news items. Some 500 copies of the first edition were sold at two pence each. The magazine was produced usually twice a year until the early 1980s.

One of the school's aims was to encourage the children to help people who were less fortunate than themselves and to support worthy causes. This was seen as an important part of their education. Charity-fund raising was partly organised through the year groups but there were also events in which all year groups were invited to take part. In 1972-73 the 2nd years decided to pay for the training of a guide dog for the blind. Within three weeks they had already raised £180 towards the £250 cost. The same year group adopted a children's home in Edinburgh and in July 1973 dispatched four large crates of toys and games. In October when they were in the 3rd year they sent a further crate, this time containing new clothing, together with £100. Two of the girls in the year were invited to spend a week at the home. The fourth-year group in June 1975 held a sponsored pram race with the aim of raising £200, part of which was to go to the Alderman Jackson appeal to provide a hydro-therapy pool and part to the Sandcastle Holiday homes in Hunstanton. According to the head of year, Mr W Ferguson, 'the races were exciting and indeed in some cases hair-raising, providing plenty of thrills for the spectators and spills for the participants.' He said that the slowest part of the event proved to be the collection of money! There were also some first-year and staff

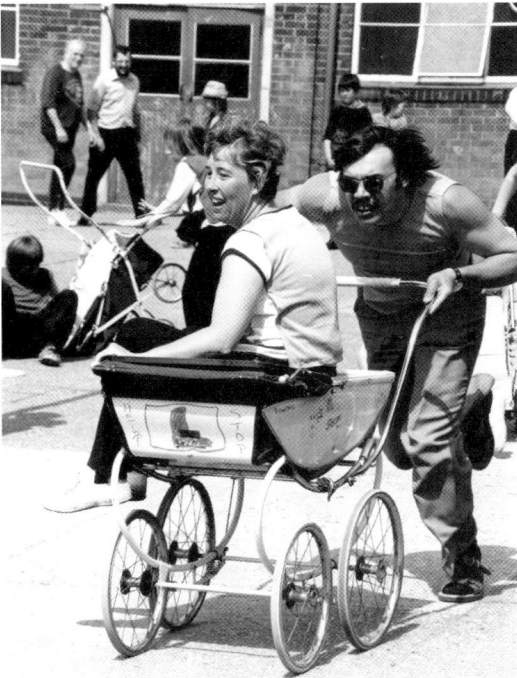

Mr Belfield and Miss Betts in a pram race (June 1975)

teams entered for the pram race and the photograph shows Mr John Belfield and Miss Anne Betts clearly having fun. First-year groups regularly raised large amounts of money for good causes. In 1975-76 they contributed £300 to the Alderman Jackson appeal already mentioned and in 1977-78 they raised £263 in a sponsored work scheme, £100 of which was sent to the Children's Ward at the King's Lynn Hospital.

Over the years there were a number of whole-school fundraising events although information on the total amounts raised is not available. However we know, for example, that in 1973-74 the 1st years contributed £200 and the 4th years £95 - raised in a five-hour sponsored disco - to the school-minibus fund. To give just one other example, in 1975-76 the 2nd years raised £194 in aid of the British Heart Foundation in a sponsored swim organised by the PE Department. The following year the same children, then in the 3rd year, raised over £100, again for the BHF, in a sponsored swim.

In the Boys' School between 1970 and 1972 a large number of visits were organised to local employers such as Cooper Roller Bearings, British Sugar, Dow Chemicals, Dornay Foods and the Lynn Docks, as well as to places of more general interest such as St Margaret's Church and St Nicholas Chapel, the Lynn Museum and the Town Hall. After the schools were amalgamated trips and visits were largely though not exclusively organised for each year group separately.

Of the very large number of trips in the period from 1972 to 1979 it is only possible to mention a representative sample. One major residential trip for 1st years was to Holt Hall. Some 30 boys and girls at a time spent a week at the centre in North Norfolk studying the local environment. The aim was to take as many children as possible during the year and in 1974-75, for example, 125 children benefited from the courses at Holt Hall. The head of year reported to the governors in June 1975 that some 300 out of the 350 in the year group had taken part in one or more of the visits which had been organised to museums, art galleries, theatres, zoos, historical sites and sporting venues. Trips for the other year groups were perhaps less numerous but nevertheless offered excellent opportunities to broaden their experiences. Some examples include: a 2nd year trip to London in March 1973 when 200 children visited the Tower of London and Regent's Park Zoo; a trip on a narrow boat on the canals of the Midlands and North-west England for 24 3rd years in the spring half term of 1974; a visit to France led by Mrs C Tilbury for 31 4th years in September 1974; and one to the Royal Norfolk Show for 75 5th years in June 1978.

The PE department organised trips to Wembley and other sporting venues each year. Examples included trips to see the All Blacks Rugby team play at Cambridge in 1972-73, an England versus Argentina football match in 1973-74 and a women's hockey international in 1974-75. In both 1973-74 and 1974-75 there were also trips to see the world-famous Harlem Globetrotters' basketball team. In addition PE staff led a number of ski trips such as those to Austria at Easter 1973 and

Italy in 1979. There were also trips for 4th and 5th years as part of the outdoor-pursuits course. In 1973-74 three staff took a group of 24 to Horton in Yorkshire, camping, walking and rock climbing. The following year a similar trip over ten days involved 20 pupils.

Other trips which included children from various year groups were the educational cruises. However, as in the past, these tended to attract only small numbers. The Deputy Head, Mrs P Linley, accompanied a group of 17 on a cruise to Norway and Denmark from 2 to 15 August and nine on a trip to Portugal and North Africa from 15 to 28 August, both in 1977. Mr Bob Rogers and Mrs Julia Dunne organised a number of trips abroad in the 1970s: to Ostend in Belgium in 1975; to the Rhine Valley in Germany in 1977; and to Sorrento in Italy in 1979, although Mrs Dunne did not go on this last one as she was on maternity leave. The trip to Germany in the May half term of 1977 was not without some problems. The group stayed at St Goar in the spectacular Rhine Gorge. However this turned out to be quite an experience as the river had recently flooded the town which had to be navigated by duck boards in places. The highlight of the trip was a cruise downstream to the picturesque town of Boppard. The group also saw the famous Lorelei rock, the cause of many a shipping disaster in the past, not far upstream from St Goar.

During the 1970s much discussion took place on the future pattern of secondary re-organisation in West Norfolk. The first proposal put forward by the Western Area Divisional Executive in May 1971 was that King Edward Vll School would become a post-16 centre and the other schools 11-16 comprehensives. As one might expect the staff and the governors at the other schools were against this idea and even at K.E.S. the teachers were divided, some wanting it to be a 14-18 school rather than an institution solely for post-16 students. By 1975 it was clear that the local authority planned to move to a system of 11-18 and 11-16 mixed-sex and all-ability schools in West Norfolk. Public notices were published to create 11-16 schools in Hunstanton and West Walton in the summer of 1975 and it was announced that as from I January 1976 the two separate Alderman Catleugh schools - for Boys and for Girls – would be brought under one Head, in preparation for secondary re-organisation.

In the Autumn Term of 1976 the Public Notice setting out the re-organisation proposals in the King's Lynn area was published. There were to be three 11-18 mixed comprehensive schools: Gaywood Park High School; King Edward Vll High School; and a high school formed by the amalgamation of the West Norfolk and King's Lynn High School for Girls and the Alderman Catleugh School, although the name of the school at that stage had not been decided. The proposals listed the partner-primary schools for each of the three new schools in King's Lynn and the aim was to provide a roughly equal share of the different socio-economic areas in the town and surrounding villages, so that as far as possible the three secondary schools would each have the chance to develop a fully comprehensive intake. Children at the 11-16 schools in Hunstanton, West Walton and Terrington would be able to transfer to any of the three Lynn schools or to NORCAT for post-16 education. The local authority's re-organisation scheme was finally approved by the Department of Education and Science in the spring of 1978.

Unfortunately the book containing the minutes of Gaywood Park Governors' meetings and the Headteacher's reports for the years 1977 to 1979 has not been located despite thorough searches at the school and in the County Archive Centre where the documents for earlier years have been stored. No doubt they contain details of discussions held and preparations made for the change to a comprehensive school. These would have been of great interest.

In the event Tom Shephard was at the school for just one year after the re-organisation before taking up his third headship in September 1980 at Sprowston High School in Norwich where he stayed until July 1990. He had always believed that headteachers should not stay for more than ten years in one school and he was true to his word. In January 1990 he was awarded a Ph.D. for his thesis on the pilot implementation of financial devolution at Sprowston and when he left he became Director of Local Financial Management for Norfolk schools. The fact that he was appointed as a headteacher of three Norfolk secondary schools and then to an important post in the local authority is a measure of the esteem in which he was held by the LEA for his leadership abilities and his expertise in financial management. When asked recently about his time in the various posts he said that it was at Gaywood Park that he gained most job satisfaction and he paid tribute to his 'wonderful staff.' Although the school had presented great challenges, Tom feels that it went from strength to strength during the time he was Headteacher.

A postscript

Mr C J Pearce

The history of the school after 1979 is for another book but a brief outline is set out below.

For one term, after Tom Shephard left in 1980 to take up his new headship in Norwich, Mr G N Stringer was Acting Head. He had also been in charge in the summer term of 1977 when Mr Shephard was given leave of absence to complete his work for an M.Phil. degree. The new Headteacher was Mr C J Pearce who was appointed as from 1 January 1981 and he was to lead the school until 1997 when he retired. He had previously been Head at two schools in Cornwall and he very ably tackled the major challenge of making the school fully comprehensive. When he arrived there were still 1620 pupils on the roll and it was in its second year of transition from being a secondary modern school. All year groups were comprehensive by September 1986.

In the 1997 July edition of the school newsletter, *Around the Park*, Cliff Pearce reflected on his time at the school and some of what he said is reproduced below:

'Over the years I have seen many changes in the school – in its buildings, its general environment, in its work and in the success of its pupils.

Massive building work has provided the school with the Library and Sixth Form Centre (1984), the Technology Block (1989), the Drama, Music and Careers facilities (1994) and the Business Centre (1994). During these years fifteen mobile classrooms have been removed....

The successes of our pupils have risen steadily during these years as reflected by examination results and by the large number of Sixth Form students passing on to university studies.

The school enjoys a fine reputation in a variety of sports. Our Activities Week has been a tremendous success, as has the programme of visits to theatres and other cultural events. Within school rarely a year has gone by without a school play or a musical occasion....

The report by the Ofsted inspectors late in 1995 must be a highlight in the history of the school since it recognised the tremendous work of staff and pupils of all levels of ability and in all areas of endeavour.

So, after more than sixteen years it is time for me to hand over responsibility for Gaywood Park High School to my successor, Mr David Stevens. I am sure that he will grow to like the school as much as I have. Certainly since I took up my post here I have never wanted another job – Gaywood Park is a fine school.'

A major change came in September 1998 when the name of the school was altered to *Park High School*. Mr Stevens said that in a time of positive developments in the school 'the new name reflects the new future direction of our school as we enter the new millennium....The new name also reflects the area the school serves which goes beyond King's Lynn and Gaywood in particular.'

David Stevens worked at improving the school and was the first to moot the idea of it becoming an academy. However during the school year 2003-04 his health deteriorated and the day-to-day running of the school fell to the Deputy Head, Dr Bob Rogers. Unfortunately Mr Stevens was unable to return to work and so Dr Rogers was appointed as Acting Head from October 2005. He continued in this role until he retired on 31 August 2010 after working at the school for 36 years.

The school became *The King's Lynn Academy* in September 2010, briefly under the leadership of Mrs Alison Ross. Mrs Ross left after two terms and Mr Craig Morrison was appointed Executive Principal. He was succeeded by Mr Alan Fletcher in 2017.

Appendices: school photographs

(a) The Boys' School, 1949 (1)

(a) The Boys' School, 1949 (2)

(a) The Boys' School, 1949 (3)

116

(a) The Boys' School, 1949 (4)

(b) A section from the Boys' School, 1958 (1)

(b) A section from the Boys' School, 1958 (2)

(c) The Girls' School, 1949 (1)

(c) The Girls' School, 1949 (2)

(c) The Girls' School, 1949 (3)

(c) The Girls' School, 1949 (4)

(d) The Girls' School, 1956 (1)

(d) The Girls' School, 1956 (2)

(d) The Girls' School, 1956 (3)

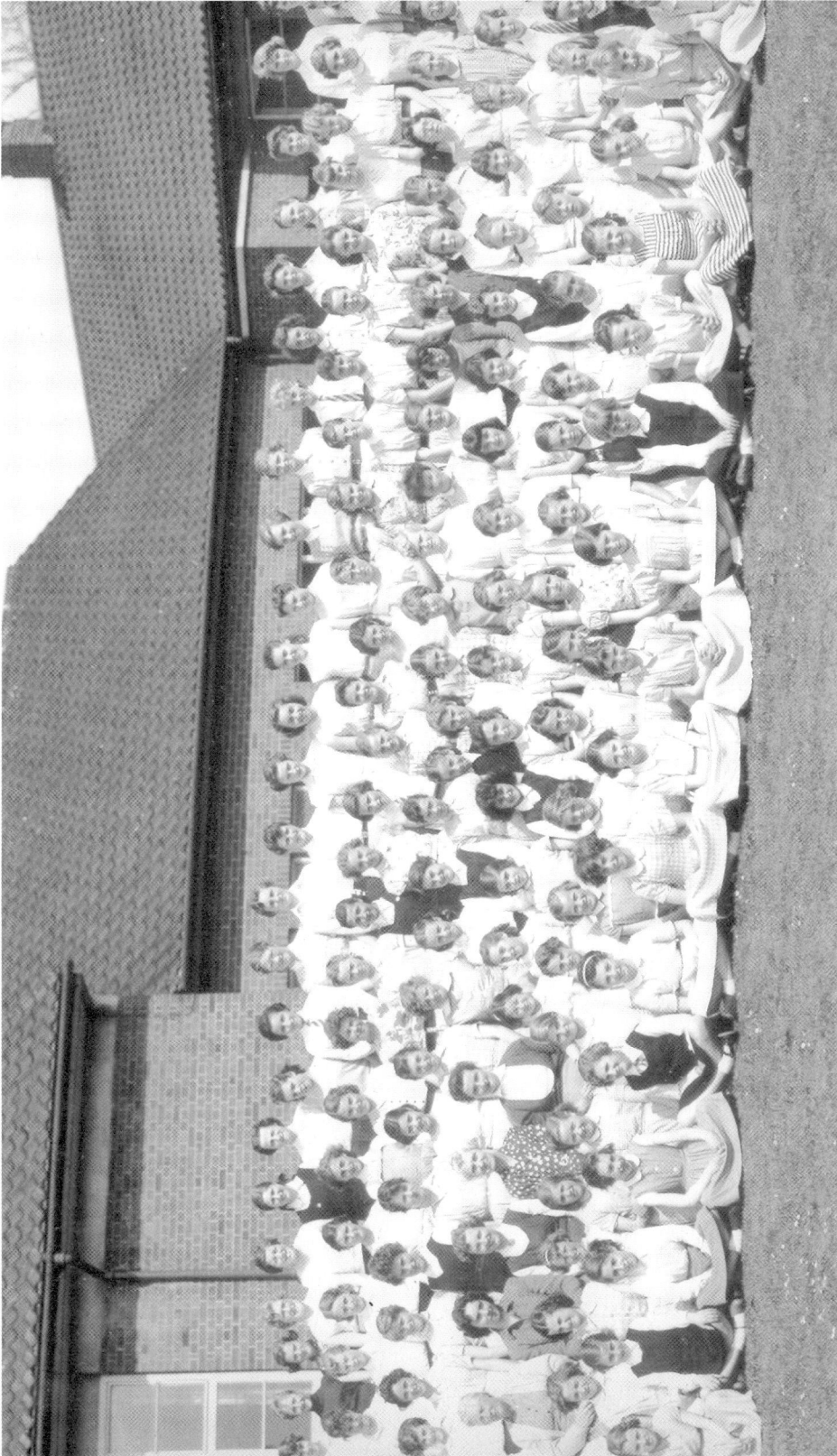

(d) The Girls' School, 1956 (4)

(d) The Girls' School, 1956 (5)

75/2

Index